W9-AAW-499

The Grill

THE ART OF

GOURMET GRILLING

THE ART OF

GOURMET GRILLING

The Grill

Karen Hendler-Kremerman

Avi Ganor

Erez Komarovsky

PRION

First published
in the United Kingdom 1991 by
PRION,
an imprint of Multimedia Books Limited,
32 - 34 Gordon House Road,
London NW5 1LP.

TEXT AND RECIPES *Karen Hendler-Kremerman*
PHOTOGRAPHY AND ART DIRECTION *Avi Ganor*
FOOD STYLIST *Erez Komarovsky*
DESIGN *Kenneth R Windsor*
EDITOR *Anne Cope*
PRODUCTION *Arnon Orbach and Hugh Allan*

Printed in Hong Kong by Imago

British Library Cataloguing in Publication Data
Hendler-Kremerman, Karen
The Grill
1. Food: Barbecue dishes - Recipes
I. Title
641.76

ISBN 1 85375 018 2

Contents

Foreword

It was Auguste Escoffier, the great French chef of the Belle Epoque, who said "We are the only animals who cook our food...and we are capable of eating when we are not hungry". But it took a Sigmund Freud, naturally, to remind us that homo sapiens *is the only species capable of turning the preparation and eating of food into a sensuous experience.*

Everyone who dines well knows that a shared meal is an occasion rich in social, sensuous and, at times, sexual messages. For me, no meal is more sensuous, either in the preparation or the eating, than one that has been prepared on the grill.

Grill cooking involves all the senses. There is a tactile pleasure in handling fresh, wholesome foods, coating them gently with oil, laying them over hot coals.... There is the hiss and sizzle of succulent meat, fish, vegetables, and fruit as they reach their peak of perfection. There are marvelous colors, patterns, and shapes.

Think too of the pleasures of eating food that has come straight from the grill. This is food as close to nature as one can get. Grilled food is a great leveller. It asks to be to be eaten with the fingers, and fingers have to be licked. I defy anyone to remain buttoned up, figuratively speaking, while trying to pry the shell off a hot grilled shrimp or the meat out of a grilled crab claw.

I love entertaining, I find enormous satisfaction in cooking, and I love cooking on the grill. The three go together beautifully. Much of my own philosophy of cooking and entertaining comes from my grandmother who, at the age of 89, still gives several large parties every year. It was from her that I learned the wisdom of the eighteenth-century French gastronome Brillat-Savarin, who said: "...to invite someone to your home is to take charge of their happiness while they are under your roof."

Happiness means a pleasant setting, good company, stimulating discussion, and good food. Welcome to my world.

Karen Hendler-Kremerman
Los Angeles, 1991

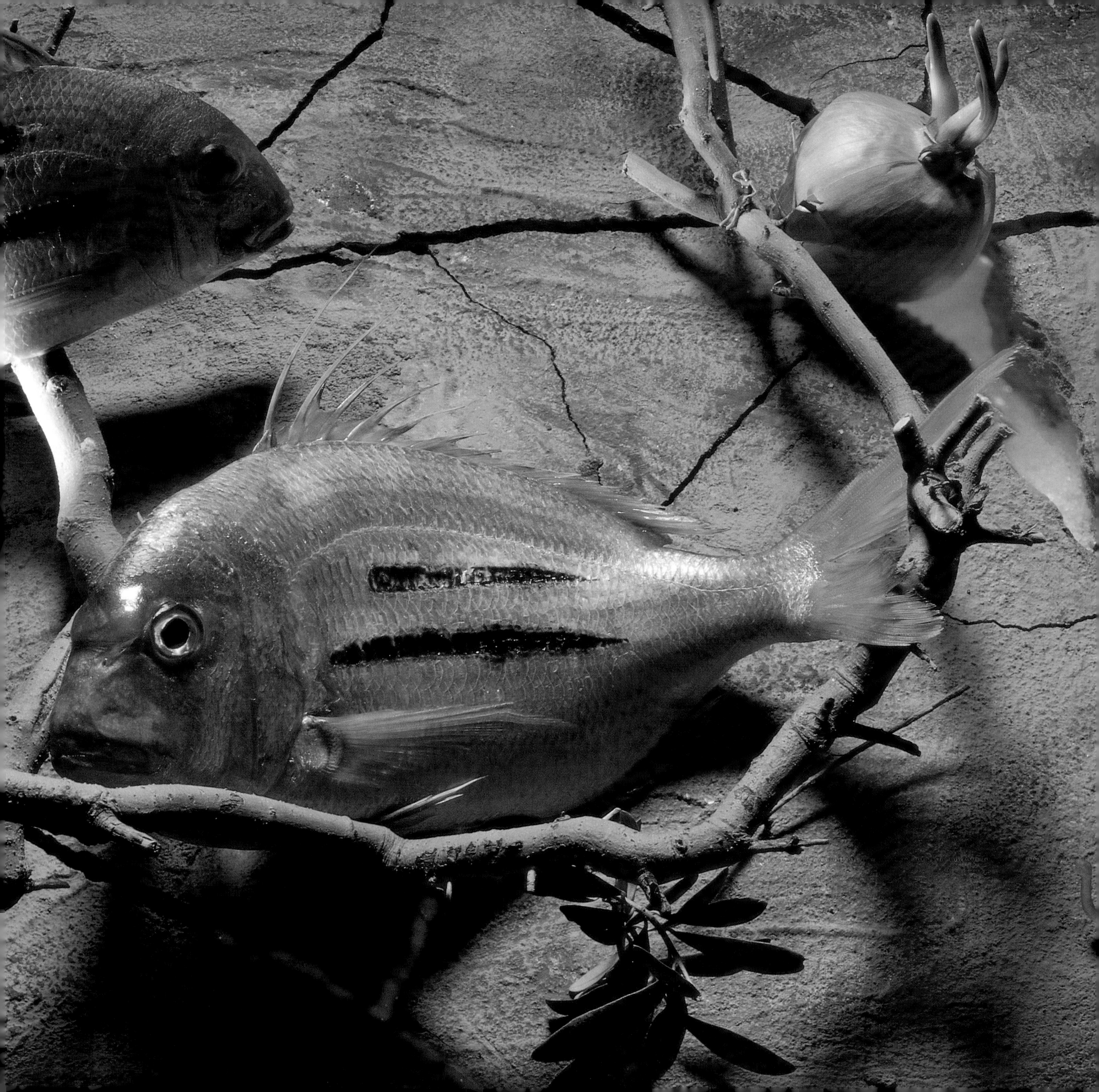

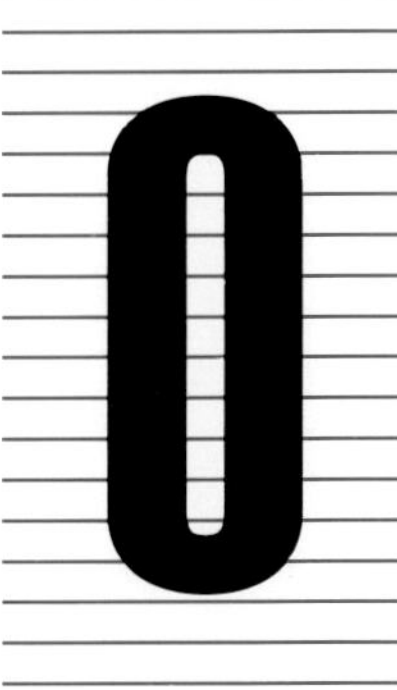

ne of the few rules I have set for myself when entertaining is this: I refuse to exile myself to the kitchen while everyone else is having a good time. If you plan a party properly you will not have to slave away in the kitchen while everyone else is admiring the sunset, flirting, gossiping, and telling jokes. This is why outdoor cooking is the ideal way to entertain.

Grill cookery is essentially simple cookery. Having prepared everything in advance, you can wait until all your guests have arrived before you begin to cook. Since you need very little equipment, there will be very little mess.

In some culinary circles, there is the insidious idea that cooking that is not complicated - or that does not cause the cook to suffer a little - is not real cooking. This is nonsense. Good food, by any standard, consists of the freshest possible ingredients cooked in a way that preserves and highlights their natural flavors, textures, and aromas. Good cooking does not attempt to disguise foods or make them taste like something they are not.

Simplicity is my watchword when entertaining. To my mind, there is no better party fare than good bread, generously brushed with olive oil, grilled over hot coals, and rubbed with garlic; artichokes, onions, and tomatoes grilled with a sprinkling of fresh herbs; freshly caught fish seasoned with salt, lemon, and herbs and grilled à point; *and fresh fruit to finish. A meal like this is a relaxed, expressive affair that everyone will enjoy.*

I prepare everything beforehand. My menus are thought out well in advance, and I start marinating the meat a day or more before the party. Several hours before my guests arrive, I cut and prepare the vegetables and fruit. On a large table next to the grill I lay out everything needed for each dish in order of use. On the same table I place the basting sauces that accompany each recipe, basting brushes, and serving dishes. I start the fire and wait for my guests. Even if they are late, there will be no agonizing over an overcooked roast, dried-out stew, or lukewarm pasta. I never start cooking until everyone is ready to eat.

There are only a few other simple guidelines that I routinely follow. I use the freshest seasonal ingredients I can find and accentuate their natural flavors with fresh herbs and simple marinades. I keep the buffet table simple and uncrowded. Quality and unfussy presentation are far more important than sheer bulk. Even a monkey can build a pile of bananas! It takes sophistication to offer a few really good dishes rather than variety for variety's sake.

A History of Pleasure

The primal pleasure of grilling a steak or spit-roasting a fish over glowing charcoal is part of an ancient tradition that goes back to the Stone Age. Today, in the age of the microchip and the microwave, the "cookout" is still a thriving institution gaining in populalarity.

Grilling probably began on that happy day some 75,000 years ago, when Paleolithic hunters discovered that meat cooked on a stone or on a wooden spit tasted considerably better than raw meat or meat tossed into the fire.

Homer's Odysseus, the wiliest of early heroes, was a great lover of outdoor cooking. One of his greatest pleasures was a wooden board groaning under huge platters of grilled meat and vegetables. After heroic deeds, heroic dining! Think of Odysseus and his crew, comfortably settled on some beach, inhaling the aroma of a roasting ox and whetting their already well-honed appetites with large quantities of wine.

There is more to such outdoor feasts than mere gustatory pleasure. To quote Odysseus: "There is no greater fulfillment of delight than when joy possesses people, and banqueters on the beach listen to a minstrel as they sit in order due, and by them the tables are laden with bread and meat right from the grill, and the cup-bearer draws wine from the bowl and pours it into the cups."

Genghis Khan also is reputed to have enjoyed the pleasures of the grill. When taking a pause from pillaging and mayhem, he liked to sit beside a stream, catch a few fish, and cook them over hot coals. When fish were not available, his other favorites were hares, sucking pigs, and wild chickens.

Nor did outdoor cooking lose its appeal as society became more "civilized." Perhaps the most extravagant feast ever prepared on the grill was the hunt luncheon given in October, 1714, by Louis XIV of France. He invited 175 members of his court to join him in a hunt on the estate of his mistress, Madame du Barry. The hunt was not remarkably successful - the bag was seven rabbits, one deer, and one boar - but Madame du Barry's chefs left nothing to chance. They had procured victuals from all over Europe - sturgeon from Russia, raw ham from Paris, wild boar from the woods near Baden-Baden, speckled trout from England, caviar from the Caspian, huge lobsters from the Adriatic, crabs from Marseilles, and deer from the Tyrolean Alps. Among the cornucopia of delicacies brought in for the occasion were white truffles from the hills of Tuscany, artichokes from Burgundy, asparagus from Normandy, wild lettuces from Provence, sweet yellow peppers from Epernay, and tomatoes specially grown for the king in the city of Nancy. The fruits included oranges from Valencia, strawberries and blackberries from the Bois de Boulogne, pineapples from the Caribbean, and mangoes from the South Pacific.

Large grills were set up on the terraces of the du Barry château, and each of the foods (with the exception of the berries, which were served raw with sweetened cream) was cooked over hot coals. The catering staff consisted of 22 chefs, 35 assistant chefs, 240 serving maids, and 120 pages.

Several years laters, as if to prove that the English also knew how to enjoy themselves, Philip Dormer Stanhope, Fourth Earl of Chesterfield, invited 1,245 guests to celebrate the birthday of his daughter. Three days before the feast, eight large pits were dug in the grounds of the castle and filled with huge quantities of oak, birch, and maple wood. Fires were started in the pits, and by the night before the feast the wood had been reduced to glowing embers.

According to historian Reay Tannahill, Lord Chesterfield's guests feasted for more than 16 hours. They devoured 25 sides of beef, 125 whole hogs, 22 wild boars, 180 each of pheasants, guinea hens, wild turkeys, and pigeons, 640 trout, and "22 wagonsful of vegetables and fruits, all of which had been prepared on spits over the open pits or on small grills which had been decoratively spread over several acres of the lawn."

Not many of us today can entertain on castle lawns, but the range of foods available to us would have reduced even a French king to stunned silence. Whatever the surroundings, and whether the menu is simple or elaborate, food cooked outdoors always has a special zest. Even in the heart of winter one can set a small grill on a balcony or just outside the kitchen door. Anyone fortunate enough to have a wood-burning fireplace will soon learn that it takes only minutes to improvise a grill right in the living room.

Some Fine (and not-so-fine) Distinctions

You can choose from five basic methods of cooking food outdoors: grilling, barbecuing, spit-cooking, pot-cooking, and smoke-cooking.

***Grilling**, the method used in this book, can be defined as cooking over the direct heat of hot coals with the food resting on a metal lattice or grid. This can be* *accomplished in a variety of ways - you can make a fire in a shallow hole in the ground and lay a metal grid over it, as is popular in Europe; or opt for a "hibachi," kettle, trolley, brick, gas, or electric grill.*

Probably the most popular method of al fresco *cooking in the Western world, grilling is an excellent method for cooking steaks, chops, patties of ground (minced) meat, fowl that have been split open to allow quick heat penetration, and skewered items such as kebabs and shashliks. Grilling also is suitable for whole fish up to about 3 lbs (1.5 kg), fish fillets, fish steaks, and a host of whole or cut vegetables and fruits.*

The great advantage of grilling is its simplicity and the fact that food cooks quickly. The drawback is that large cuts of meat cannot be cooked satisfactorily unless a great deal of care is taken to prevent the outside getting burnt to a cinder.

Barbecuing*, in the precise sense of the term, is nearly impossible unless you have three things: a great deal of space, a great deal of wood (not charcoal), and a great deal of time. Although the word "barbecue" has come to be used loosely to describe all forms of outdoor cooking, a real barbecue requires a large fire in a pit, burned down to produce a bed of coals at least 12 inches (30 cm) thick. Large pieces of meat are anointed with a spicy sauce based on chili peppers and tomatoes, wrapped in wet burlap, laid on the coals, and cooked under the earth for as long as 24 hours. Quite an undertaking! This style of cooking is not practical for the average family cookout.*

Spit-cooking, pot-cooking, and smoke-cooking are other methods of cooking over hot coals. Although the recipes in this book do not use these methods, they are defined briefly as a matter of interest.

Spit-cooking requires a stream of superheated air from the cooking coals to be directed over and around the food, which is skewered with a revolving spit. The food on the spit cooks evenly and requires frequent basting.

Spit-cooking *is most suitable for large cuts of meat. Its limitation is that some kind of power is required to keep the spit turning. Spits can, of course, be turned by hand, but most people find it impractical. Greeks, Turks, and many Middle Eastern people enjoy spit-cooking whole lambs or goats. U. S. President Lyndon Johnson thrived on holding parties for 100 or more guests and spit-cooking whole hogs and sides of beef.*

Pot-cooking*, also called Dutch oven cooking, is suitable for foods that must be cooked in liquid (stews, pot roasts, pulses, and the like). It involves extra equipment, large amounts of fuel, and long cooking times. Of all the methods of cooking involving the use of hot coals, this is the most closely related to indoor cooking. Many Japanese and Koreans are fond of pot-cooking.*

Smoke-cooking *is the ancient Chinese version of barbecuing. The method is still used in parts of China and Korea. A large barrel-shaped clay oven is buried in the earth, meat or other items are suspended on wires or laid loosly on a lattice inside it, and the heat is supplied by a miniature fire of aromatic wood. Bona fide smoke-cooking requires an almost airtight oven and great patience - cooking can take as long as two or three weeks. Today many people paint their meat with a chemical concoction known as "liquid smoke" and turn up the heat to shorten the cooking time. The results of such shortcuts are usually unfortunate.*

Basic Equipment

There is no need to spend a fortune on the "ultimate" grill. The art of grilling is the sympathetic preparation of the food you put on the grill - not the grill equipment you use.

Gas and electric grills have advantages. They light at the touch of a button and heat the "coals" - usually pieces of lava or ceramic rock - in less than 10 minutes. After that, the heat can be regulated by turning a dial.

But for the simplest (and often the best) grilling, all you need is a brazier to hold coals, a grid on which to place the food, tongs for turning and serving, and brushes for basting.

To these essentials one might add some sort of fire-tending implement (a rake or poker), a spray bottle or squirt gun to douse flare-ups caused by fat dripping onto the coals, and a sandwich-style grid (a pair of grids, in fact, with a handle on one side and hinges on the other) to make turning easier. If you spear meat or fish with a fork when turning them, the juices escape, and with them much of the flavor. If you do not have a sandwich-style grid, turn the food with tongs. (All grilling implements should have long handles, for obvious reasons). If you buy metal skewers, make sure they are rectangular in cross-section. Bamboo or wooden skewers should be soaked in water for an hour or so before use to prevent them splintering.

An Abundance of Delectable Choices

Too many outdoor cooks limit their efforts to the obvious or uninteresting - hamburgers, hot dogs, sausages, and "shish kebabs." Yet there are countless other foods, many of them inexpensive and equally easy to prepare, that can transform a dull meal into a sparkling feast.

The first category of food that comes to mind is meat. The choices in this category are almost limitless: beef, lamb, veal, and pork. The same is true for poultry, fish, and seafood. All can be prepared over the same coals without adding complexity to the cooking. Also, when composing a menu, consider variety meats such as kidneys, liver, heart, and brains.

Many vegetables have a special affinity for the outdoor grill or spit. These include potatoes, yams, eggplants (aubergines), zucchini (courgettes), okra, peppers, sweet corn, onions, carrots, fennel, mushrooms, tomatoes, and globe artichokes.
A number of fruits are particularly appropriate for outdoor cooking - dates, apples, pears, papayas (pawpaws), and peaches are especially rewarding.

Civilized Simplicity

Enjoyable grilled food need not be fancy - quite the opposite! Complicated recipes belong in the kitchen. Yet simplicity does not mean that civilized touches should be eliminated.

Many delicious sauces and marinades for grilled foods can be prepared with a minimum of time, ingredients, and utensils. A flavorful oil, marinade, or sauce can transform an ordinary cut of meat into a gourmet dish.

Many foods benefit from being marinated before cooking. A marinade acts as a tenderizer and contributes extra flavor. Marinating times, which can vary from 1 hour to several days, are suggested for each recipe in this book.

One of the tricks of really good grill cookery is basting, the use of oil, reserved marinade juices, sauces, or pan drippings to keep the food moist and succulent.

For making marinades and basting liquids, the basic ingredients are usually oil, vinegar, and lemon juice. Olive oil is popular in many parts of the world, but safflower or peanut oil has a more subtle flavor. Corn and cottonseed oil should not be used for grilling, as they contain additives which leave a bitter taste.

Eventually you may decide to keep on hand several types of flavored oil for basting. One of the most useful is spiced oil. You can make a spiced oil by half filling a jar or bottle with dried red chili peppers and a few crushed cloves of garlic, then filling with olive oil. To make rosemary-flavored oil, loosely fill a jar with fresh sprigs of rosemary, add a few crushed garlic cloves, and top off with olive oil. Flavored oils should be allowed to stand, well sealed, for a week or so before using. This time allows them to develop their full flavor. Tightly sealed, they can be stored almost indefinitely.

As for vinegars, wine vinegars are invariably more subtle than malt vinegars. Sherry, cider, champagne, fruit, balsamic, and herbed vinegars offer a wide range of taste possibilities. Herbed vinegars are easy to make at home. Start with a high quality wine vinegar, add fresh herbs, seal, and wait three weeks before using.

The best salt for outdoor cookery is coarse salt (sold as sea salt or rock salt), and the best pepper is freshly ground. Other flavorings in the grill box might include sage, basil, thyme, rosemary, bay, oregano, savory, paprika, and cayenne pepper. If chicken is a favorite of yours, include tarragon, and if you plan to prepare fish frequently, add dill. Fresh herbs are nearly always better than dried.

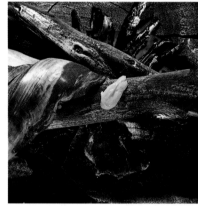

Over Glowing Coals

In grilling, the operative world is "coals" or "heat" rather than "fire." Food cooked over flame burns on the outside and remains raw inside (and the cook is likely to suffer from well-done eyebrows).

Grilling should be done over a bed of glowing - not flaming - charcoal. Ready-made charcoal is easy to buy, but the most rewarding way of grilling food is to start with dry wood and make your own charcoal from a wood fire. Build the fire and light it about 2 hours before you plan to start cooking. Let the fire burn freely, adding more wood as necessary, until it reduces to embers. For grilling you need a bed of embers 2 - 3 inches (5 - 8 cm) thick and as long and wide as the grill rack you are using. For spit-cooking, the bed of embers should be about 4 - 6 inches (10 - 15 cm) deep, with the edges of the embers extending about 2 inches (5 cm) beyond the area directly beneath the food. Allow space directly under the spit for a drip pan.

Commercial charcoal is wood that has been burned to remove the sap and lignins, then crushed and compressed into pellets or briquettes of uniform size and density. Except for the first few moments after it is lighted, commercial charcoal emits neither smoke nor flame.

Safety Always

Whether you are using a simple hibachi or an elaborate gas barbecue, make sure that your grill is in a stable position.

Never pour flammable liquid - kerosene, methylated spirits, or paraffin - on any coals. All lighting fuel should be used according to the manufacturer's instructions.

If you cook food over charcoal that is still flaming or burning, it will taste unpleasant. Keep a spray bottle handy for dousing flare-ups, and make sure all your implements have long handles. Keep a thick pair of oven mitts handy, too.

If possible, buy charcoal that has been impregnated with an oil that makes it easy to light. The fumes and odor from the oil dissipate long before the coals are hot enough to cook on. Alternatively, use a naptha-based "quick starter" - there are many brands on the market. Don't be tempted to use gasoline as a starter. It has a high flash point and is extremely dangerous.

Let Grilling Commence

If you are using commercial charcoal, start the fire about 40 minutes before you plan to start cooking. While the coals are heating, they should be blown or fanned until the top layers begin to burn. After that, keep adding lumps of charcoal until there is enough for the cooking you plan to do. Keep the bed of coals compact and the burning briquettes in close contact.

You will know when your coals are ready by their color. In bright sunlight they will appear gray; in shade they will look reddish-gray; at dusk or in the dark they will glow a rich, deep red. At this point, spread them out over an area equal to the grill rack. Then oil the grill to prevent food from sticking.

This is the time to take advantage of the delicious aromas of fruitwood chips (peach, grape, citrus, apple, hickory, or mesquite) or bundles of fresh herbs. Soak the chips or herbs in water before adding them to the coals; this produces fragrant smoke, not flames.

Grilling temperatures - high, medium, or low - are given for each recipe in this book, but knowing when your coals have reached the right temperature is a matter of experience. Briquettes, for example, do not glow dull red like charcoal when they are hot; when they are ready to cook on they are covered with a fine gray ash. Charcoal which has reached the gray ash stage is no longer hot.

Most meat, poulty, and fish cook best if you let them come to room temperature first, but cook them immediately afterwards. When grilling meat, sear it first over a high heat to seal in the juices, then move it to a cooler part of the grill to finish cooking. Cooking heat can be lowered by increasing the distance between the grill and the coals, or by spacing out the coals.

Once you have begun to cook, do not fan, blow on, or stir the coals, unless you enjoy the taste of ashes. To make the coals burn hotter after cooking has begun, tap them with a long stick. This dislodges surface ash and allows fresh air to reach them. Where a low cooking heat is required, allow the coals to become coated with ash.

Once your bed of coals has reached the right temperature, it can be kept hot by adding preheated coals (5 - 10 coals every 30 minutes for a fairly small grill). Always keep 10 - 15 fresh coals at the edge of the grill for this purpose; or, if you prefer, keep a small extra fire going in a hibachi.

There is no need to waste hot coals. Plan so that when most of your cooking is finished you can use the fire to prepare one or more items for the next day. Grilled hamburgers and many other meats are delicious served cold with a piquant sauce; cold grill-ed trout is a superb treat when served with a good mayonnaise; fruit that has been grilled and chilled is delicious with sweetened whipped cream. After you have finished cooking, leave the charcoal to burn out.

N*ever forget that grill cookery is meant to be casual, easy, and fun. More than any other mode of cooking, grilling encourages experimentation. Just because a recipe calls for red wine vinegar or basil does not mean that lemon juice and oregano will not do just as well. In other words, follow your hunches - and savor the rewards of the art of grilling.*

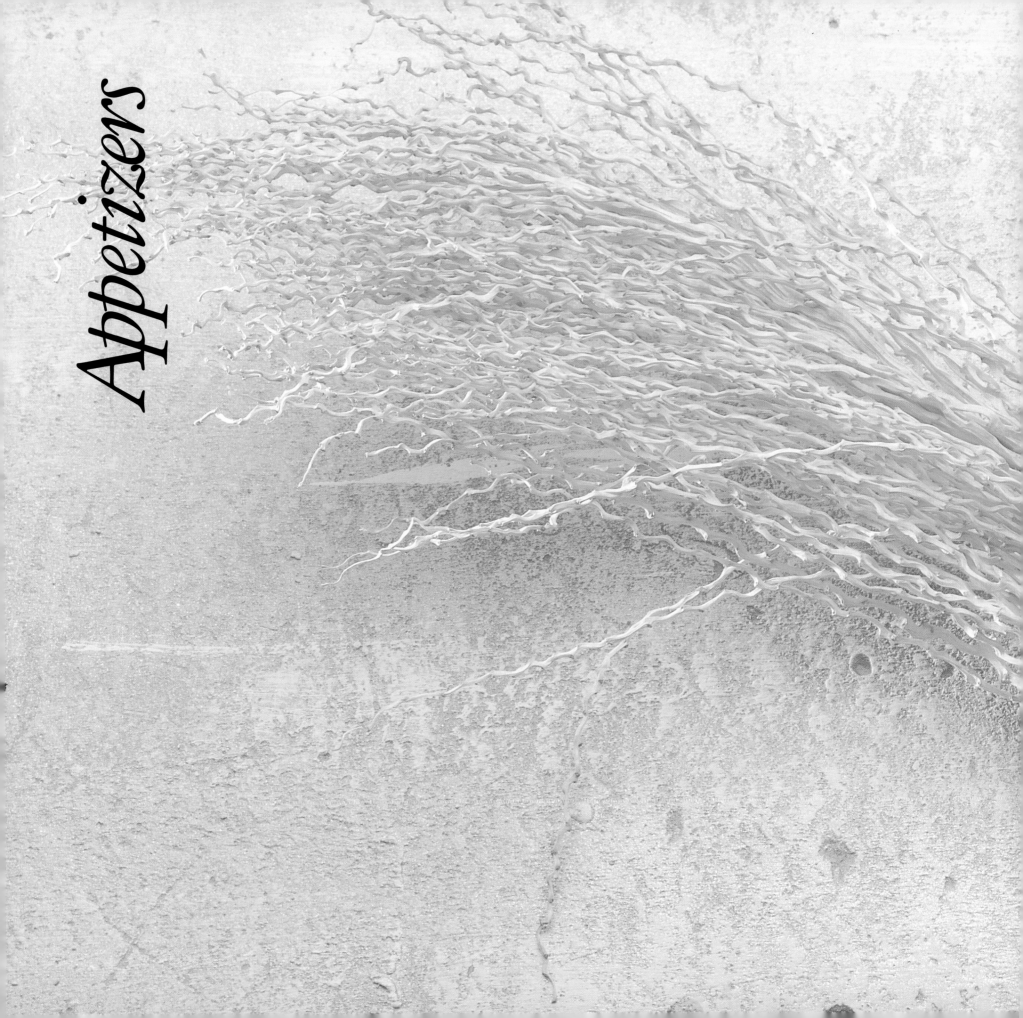

Appetizers

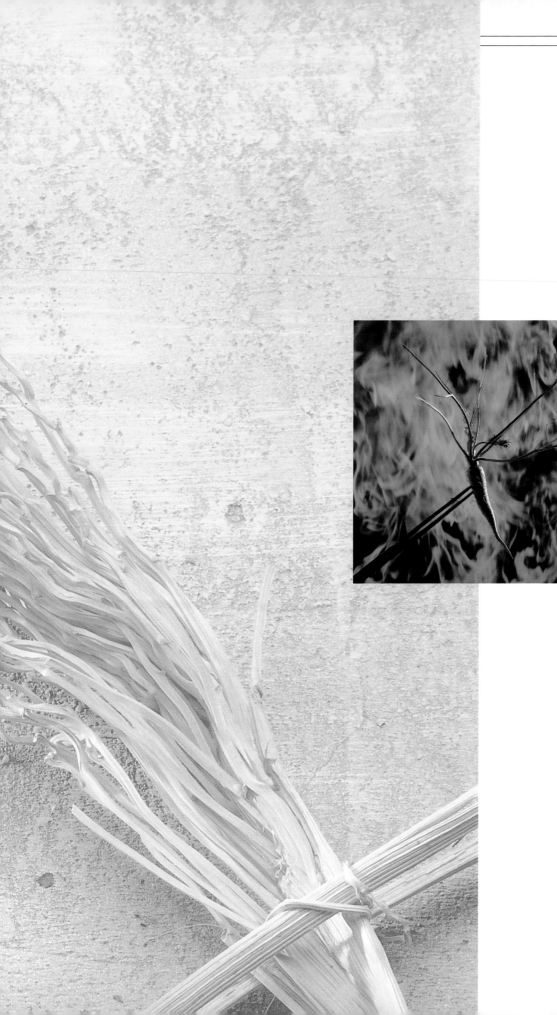

THERE WAS A LONG TABLE SET WITH SO MANY DIFFERENT SORTS OF APPETIZERS THAT WE DID NOT KNOW WHERE TO START OR WHERE TO FINISH. EVERYTHING LOOKED DELICIOUS, SMELLED MARVELLOUS AND TASTED EVEN BETTER. BEFORE LONG WE HAD RETURNED TO FILL OUR PLATES TWO, THREE, FOUR TIMES AND BY THE TIME THE WAITER CAME TO TAKE OUR ORDER WE FOUND THAT WE HAD ALREADY STUFFED OURSELVES QUITE NICELY.

Mark Twain

American writer and humorist

(1835 - 1910)

CHAPTER ONE

Appetizers

Although hors d'oeuvres are generally thought of as ethereal offerings to tickle the reluctant palate before dining begins in earnest, there is no reason why an entire menu should not be composed of appetizers.

❦ *As an introduction to a full meal I serve at least two different appetizers, making sure that each guest has at least three portions of each offering. There is no better way for people to settle in before dinner than by holding a drink in one hand and an appetizer in the other. For cocktail parties or dinners based entirely on appetizers, I prepare six, eight, or more different dishes.*

❦ *Whether preparing food for six, twenty, or two hundred people, make sure your appetizers have an interesting variety of colors, textures, and sauces, and don't hesitate to offer novel combinations of meat, fish, vegetables, and fruit. Especially in planning large parties, remember that all your principal ingredients can be cut, marinated, and skewered in advance.*

RECIPES

Appetizers

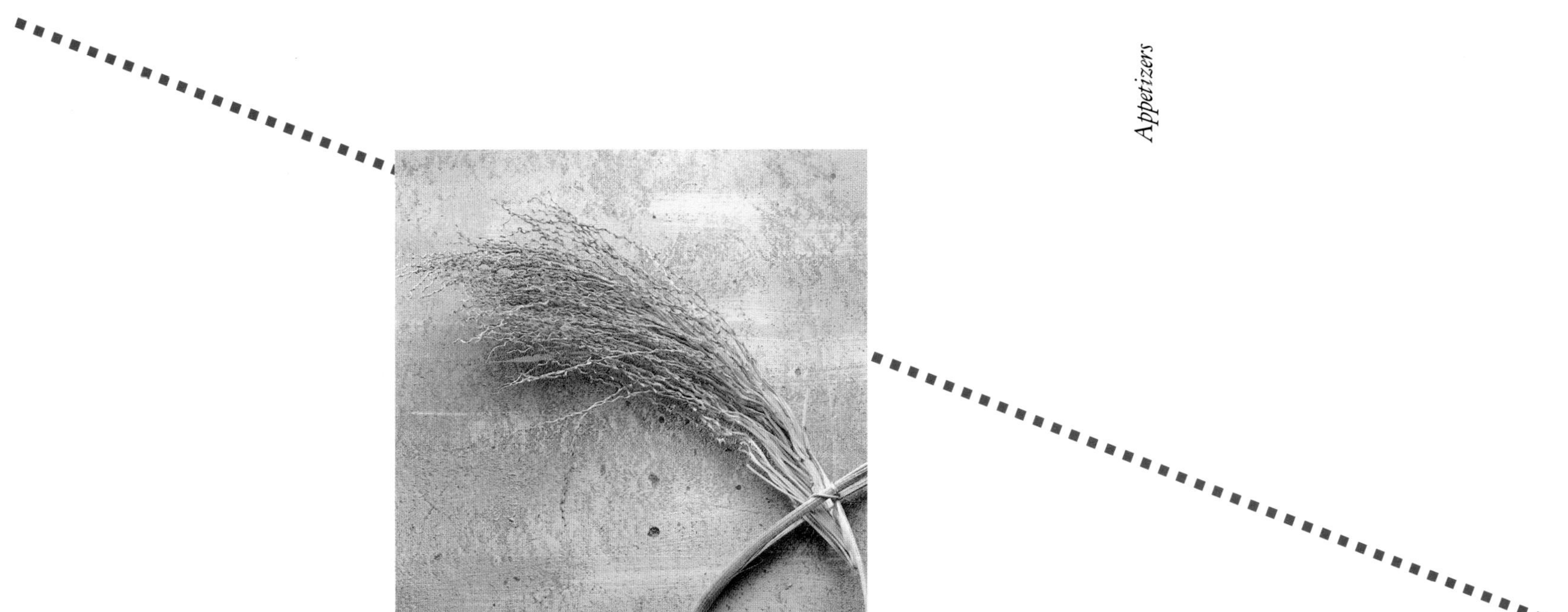

SKEWERS OF SALMON

- 1 lb / 450 g fillet of fresh salmon
- 1 tablespoon coarse salt
- 1 1/2 tablespoons sugar
- olive oil
- fresh herbs such as dill, basil, or tarragon
- soaked bamboo skewers

1 *Sprinkle the flesh side of the fillet with salt and sugar. Lightly oil a platter and strew herbs in the bottom. Lay the fish, flesh side down, on top of the herbs. Cover with a damp cloth and refrigerate for 24 hours.*

2 *Take the salmon out of the herb, salt, and sugar mixture and cut it into large cubes or into thick slices as long as your thumb. Thread one or two cubes or one slice on each bamboo skewer and lightly brush with olive oil. Place the skewers on the grill over a medium heat and cook for 1 minute, turning the skewers after 30 seconds. The fish should remain rare and succulent inside.*

❦ **SERVES 6** AS AN APPETIZER OR **4** AS A MAIN DISH

SWORDFISH SKEWERS

- 1/2 cup / 100 ml olive oil
- 1 teaspoon freshly ground pepper
- 1 lb / 450 g swordfish, cut into slices 1 inch / 2.5 cm thick
- soaked bamboo skewers
- fresh lime juice

1 *Toss the swordfish slices in the olive oil and pepper. Marinate for several hours.*

2 *Thread the slices onto skewers and cook for 1/2 minute on each side over a medium heat. Season with salt and a squeeze of fresh lime juice.*

❦ **SERVES 6** AS AN APPETIZER OR **3** AS A MAIN COURSE

ZHOUG RELISH

THIS IS A HOT RELISH POPULAR IN THE MIDDLE EAST. IT ADDS PEP TO SOUPS, SAUCES, AND STEWS.

- 15 - 20 hot fresh chili peppers, or more to taste
- 15 - 20 large cloves garlic
- 4 - 5 cups fresh coriander
- 4 teaspoons cumin
- 1 1/2 teaspoons salt
- 1 tablespoon freshly ground pepper

1 *Put all the ingredients in a food processor and blend to a coarse paste. Taste and adjust the seasoning if necessary.*

❦ **MAKES ABOUT 1 CUP / 225 ml**

MUSHROOMS STUFFED WITH FRESH HERBS

- 18 large brown or wild mushrooms, caps only

STUFFING

- 1 cup flat-leaved parsley, finely chopped
- 1/2 cup fresh mint, finely chopped
- 2 - 4 tablespoons Zhoug Relish (see recipe below left)
- 1/2 - 1 teaspoon coarse salt
- olive oil

1 *Clean the mushrooms with a damp cloth and make several slits in the thickest part of each cap.*

2 *Mix together the stuffing ingredients. Put a little stuffing in the slits and the rest into the caps. Brush with a little olive oil.*

3 *Place the mushrooms on the grill, cap side up. Cook over a medium heat for 3 - 5 minutes or until the mushrooms are hot and soft. Serve hot from the grill or at room temperature.*

❦ **SERVES 6** AS AN APPETIZER OR SIDE DISH

PAPAYA SKEWERS WITH CHILI LIME BUTTER

CHILI LIME BUTTER

- 1/2 cup / 100 g butter, melted
- 2 dried or fresh red chili peppers, chopped
- juice and grated zest of 1 lime
- salt and freshly ground pepper

- 1 1/2 lbs/ 700 g firm papaya (pawpaw), peeled, seeded, and cut into 2-inch / 5-cm cubes
- soaked bamboo skewers

1 *Melt the butter and stir in the chili peppers, lime juice, and zest. Season to taste with salt and pepper.*

2 *Toss the papaya pieces in the chili lime butter. Thread each papaya piece onto the end of a bamboo skewer.*

3 *Place the skewers on the grill and cook over a medium heat, basting with the remaining butter, until just golden.*

❦ **SERVES 6**

CHILI PRAWNS WITH CORIANDER DIPPING SAUCE

- 1 lb / 450 g large prawns (about 12 if really large)

MARINADE

- juice of 1 lemon
- juice of 4 limes
- 3 cloves garlic, coarsely chopped
- 4 small hot fresh chili peppers, coarsely chopped
- 1/2 teaspoon coarse salt

- olive oil
- 4 tablespoons chopped fresh coriander
- freshly ground pepper

1 *Remove the heads and legs of the prawns, leaving the shell intact.*

2 *Mix together the marinade ingredients and pour over the prawns. Marinate for 3 - 4 hours.*

3 *Drain the prawns and reserve the marinade. Toss the prawns in enough olive oil to coat them. Place on a grill over a medium heat and cook for 3 - 4 minutes, depending on size, turning occasionally and basting with more olive oil.*

4 *Add a little olive oil to the reserved marinade and season with pepper to taste. Stir in the coriander and serve as a dipping sauce.*

❦ **SERVES 6** AS AN APPETIZER OR **3** AS A MAIN DISH

SKEWERS OF CHICKEN OR PORK SOUTHEAST-ASIAN STYLE

MARINADE

- 3 cloves garlic
- 4 scallions (green or spring onions), white part only
- 1 - 2 fresh chili peppers, seeded and coarsely chopped
- 1 1/2 teaspoons sugar
- 1/2 cup fresh coriander, or fresh coriander and fresh basil mixed
- 1/2 teaspoon freshly ground pepper
- 1 - 2 tablespoons nuoc mam (Vietnamese fish sauce, sold in most Chinese stores)
- 1 - 2 tablespoons soy sauce

- 1 lb / 450 g boneless chicken breasts, skinned and cut into 1-inch / 2.5-cm cubes **OR** 1 lb / 450 g pork tenderloin, cubed
- 2 tablespoons vegetable or olive oil
- soaked bamboo skewers

SOUTHEAST-ASIAN SAUCE

- 3 cloves garlic crushed
- 1/2 tablespoon minced fresh ginger, optional
- 2 tablespoons sugar
- 3 tablespoons fresh lime or lemon juice
- 3 tablespoons rice vinegar
- 3 tablespoons nuoc mam
- 2 tablespoons water
- 1 fresh chili pepper, seeded and thinly sliced

1 *Using a blender or food processor, combine all the marinade ingredients to a smooth paste. Add the cubed chicken or pork and toss well. Marinate for several hours or overnight.*

2 *Combine the ingredients for the Southeast-Asian sauce, stirring until the sugar has dissolved.*

3 *Before grilling, brush the meat with the olive oil. Thread two pieces of meat onto each skewer and cook over a high heat for 2 - 3 minutes on each side. Serve with the Southeast-Asian sauce.*

❦ **SERVES 6** AS AN APPETIZER OR **3** AS A MAIN DISH

SKEWERED CHICKEN WITH SCALLIONS OR CHERRY TOMATOES

MARINADE

- 2 tablespoons olive or vegetable oil
- 2 tablespoons dry sherry
- 2 cloves garlic, minced
- 3 tablespoons soy sauce
- 1 tablespoon grated zest of lemon or lime
- 2 tablespoons fresh lemon or lime juice

- 1 lb / 450 g chicken breast, boned and cut into 1-inch / 2.5-cm cubes
- 20 cherry tomatoes OR scallions (green or spring onions)
- soaked bamboo skewers

1 *Mix together the marinade ingredients, pour over the cubes of chicken, and toss well. Marinate for at least 3 hours.*

2 *Remove the chicken cubes from the marinade. Reserve the marinade. Thread one or two cubes of chicken, and one cherry tomato or scallion (cut on the diagonal into 2 inch / 5 cm pieces), onto each skewer.*

3 *Place the skewers on an oiled grill over a low heat. Cook for 1 1/2 minutes on each side, basting with the marinade.*

❦ **MAKES 16 TO 20 SKEWERS**

LEMON PEPPER CHICKEN

MARINADE

- 1/2 cup / 100 ml olive oil
- 4 tablespoons lemon juice
- 2 tablespoons brandy or dry white wine
- 1/2 tablespoon freshly ground pepper
- 2 cloves garlic, chopped
- salt

- 12 small chicken thighs, wings, or drumsticks.

1 *Mix together all the marinade ingredients, pour over the chicken pieces, and mix well. Marinate for at least 4 hours or overnight.*

2 *Remove the chicken pieces from the marinade and season with a little more salt. Place on the grill over a medium heat and cook for about 6 minutes on each side, basting well with the marinade. Serve hot or at room temperature.*

❦ **SERVES 6** AS AN APPETIZER OR **4** AS A MAIN DISH

SKEWERS OF FOIE GRAS

- 1 lb / 450 g foie gras (goose liver)
- olive oil
- salt and freshly ground pepper
- soaked bamboo skewers

1 *Cut the liver into 1-inch / 2.5-cm pieces, brush with olive oil, and season with salt and pepper. Thread each piece onto the end of a skewer.*

2 *Place the skewers on an oiled grill over a medium hot heat and cook for about 1 minute on each side.*

❦ **MAKES ABOUT 20 SKEWERS**

FIGS WITH PROSCIUTTO

- 10 firm fresh figs, halved
- 20 paper-thin slices of prosciutto (Parma ham), Westphalian ham, or lachs schinken
- 4 tablespoons melted butter
- soaked bamboo skewers

1 *Wrap each half fig in a slice of prosciutto and put on the end of a skewer.*

2 *Place the skewers on the grill over a medium heat and baste with the melted butter. Cook for3 - 5 minutes.*

❦ **MAKES 20 SKEWERS**

SCALLIONS WITH MUSTARD BUTTER

MUSTARD BUTTER

- 5 tablespoons melted butter
- 2 tablespoons Dijon mustard
- 1 tablespoon lemon juice
- salt and freshly ground pepper

- 20 large scallions (green or spring onions)
- soaked bamboo skewers

1 *Combine the mustard butter ingredients and season to taste with salt and pepper.*

2 *Trim the scallions so that they are about 5 inches / 12 cm long and thread them lengthwise onto bamboo skewers. Grill over a medium heat for 4 - 5 minutes until well browned, basting from time to time with the mustard butter.*

❦ **MAKES 20 SKEWERS**

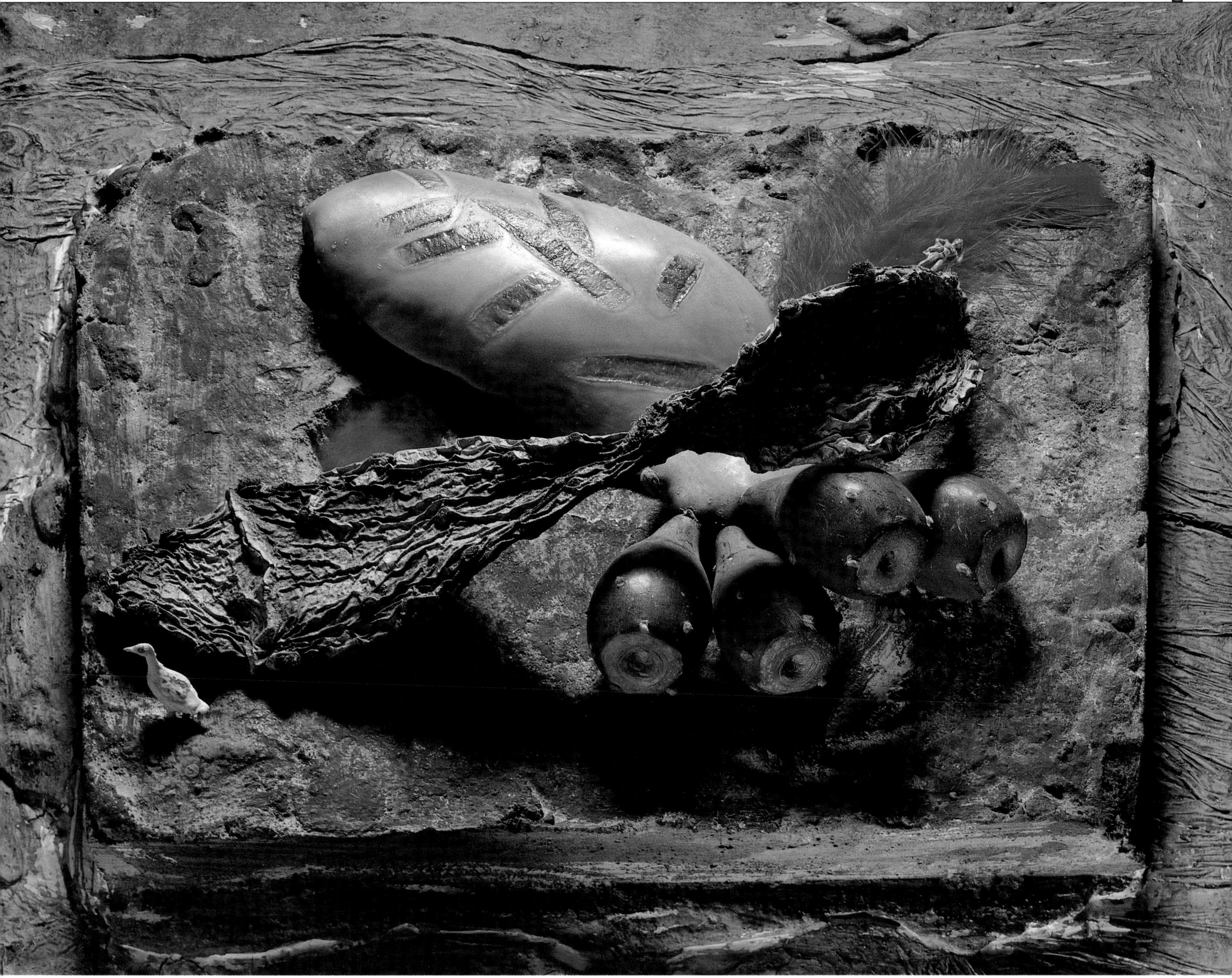

1

BRUSCHETTE VERSION 1

12 slices good crusty bread about 1 1/2 inches / 4 cm thick
5 cloves garlic, lightly crushed
1 large tomato, cut in half
olive oil

1 *Grill the bread until light grill marks appear.*

2 *Quickly rub one side of each slice with the garlic and tomato. Place on a plate and drizzle liberally with olive oil.*

❦ **SERVES 6**

BRUSCHETTE VERSION 2

4 tomatoes, chopped
1 cup coarsely chopped fresh basil or arugala (curly endive)
salt and freshly ground pepper
6 large or 12 small slices crusty bread about 1 1/2 inches / 4 cm thick
5 cloves garlic, lightly crushed
olive oil

1 *Mix together the tomatoes, chopped herbs, salt, and pepper.*

2 *Grill the bread until light grill marks appear. Rub with garlic, top with the tomato and herb mixture, and sprinkle generously with olive oil.*

❦ **SERVES 6**

HERBED GARLIC BREAD

2 baguettes, French or sourdough
1 cup / 225 g melted butter
2 - 4 tablespoons olive oil
4 - 6 cloves garlic, minced
juice of 1/2 lemon
3 tablespoons Dijon mustard
2 1/2 cups coarsely chopped fresh herbs (a mixture of chives, basil, and parsley, for example)
salt and freshly ground pepper

1 *Slice the baguettes in half horizontally and make four cuts in each half, cutting halfway through.*

2 *Mix together all the other ingredients, adding salt and pepper to taste.*

3 *Generously brush the herbed butter on the cut side of the baguette halves. Place on an oiled grill, cut side down, and toast over a medium heat until golden brown. Turn and grill for 1 minute on the crust side. Serve hot.*

❦ **SERVES 6 TO 8**

Starters

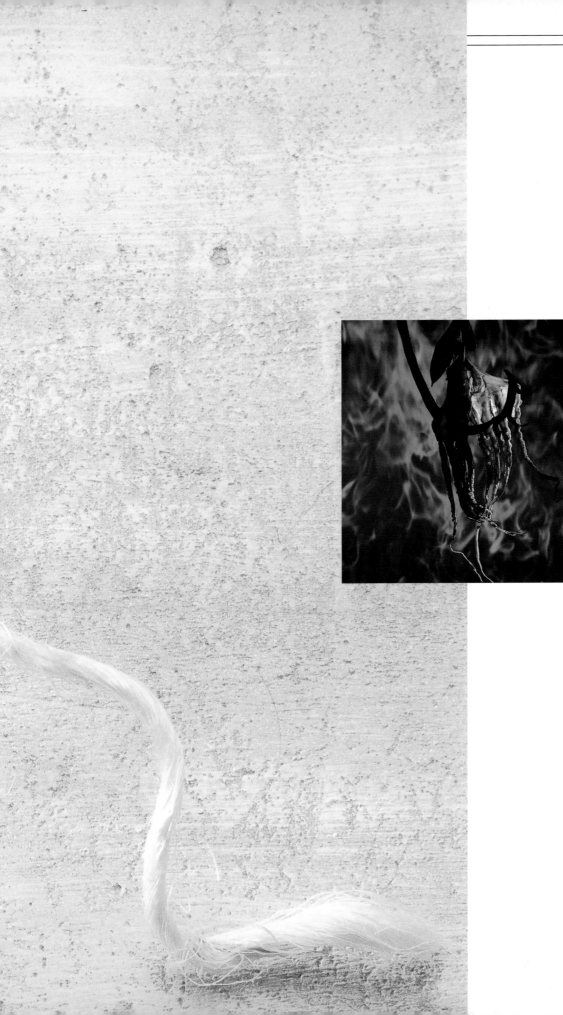

SOME SAY THESE PACIFIC ISLANDERS ARE BARBARIANS,

BUT I SAY THEY ARE MORE CIVILIZED THAN WE.

WHEN WE SAT DOWN TO DINE THEY SERVED US

OYSTERS AND CRABS, CHOICE CUTS OF MUTTON

AND PIG, BREADFRUIT, PAPAYA AND PINEAPPLES

AND A MARVELLOUS LIQUEUR MADE FROM

POMEGRANATES. TO OUR GREAT SURPRISE THIS

WAS ONLY THE FIRST COURSE OF A SIX-COURSE

DINNER....

Captain James Cook

English navigator and explorer

(1728 - 1779)

CHAPTER TWO

Starters

We shall never know if it was etiquette among Captain Cook's Pacific Islanders to choose a single dish as a first course or sample a little of everything. First courses should, as master chef Antonin Carême once said, "be the merest hint of what is to come. They should never be so filling as to deprive the diner of the pleasures of the remainder of his dinner."

❦ *Because first courses should always have a special delicacy and lightness, they give the grill chef an opportunity to master the use of spices and herbs with an eclectic range of foods. The flavors of first courses should not be so assertive that they mask the taste of what is to follow.*

❦ *By increasing the quantities, most of the recipes in this section can be promoted to main course status.*

RECIPES

Starters

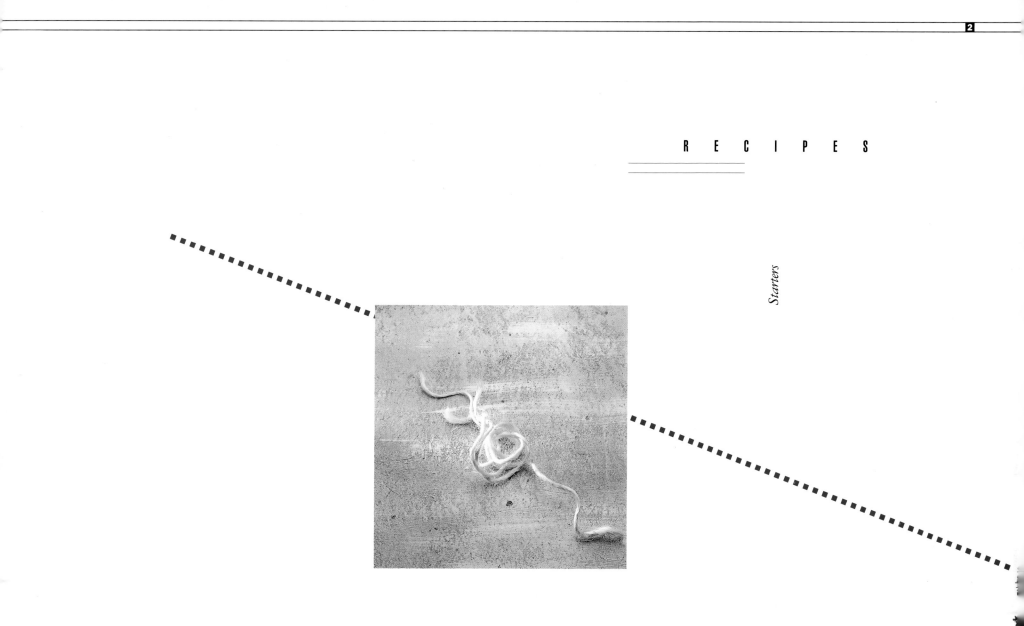

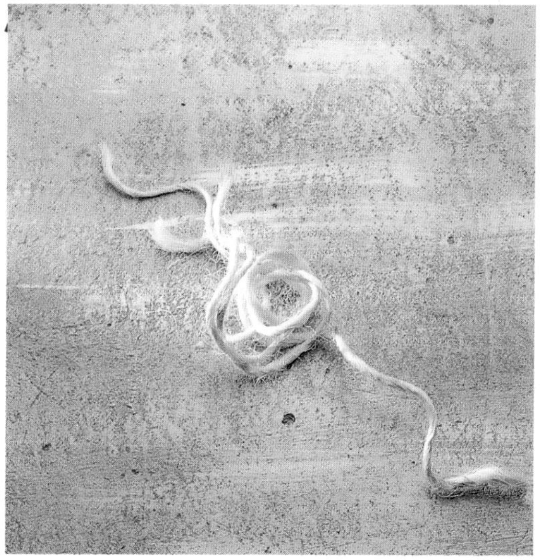

BRUSCHETTE WITH MUSHROOMS

- 20 cloves garlic
- 6 tablespoons olive oil

MARINADE

- 1 1/2 lbs / 700 g mixed mushrooms (wild, shitake, oyster, button, etc.)
- 1/2 cup / 100 ml olive oil
- 2 tablespoons sherry vinegar or wine vinegar
- salt and freshly ground pepper
- 1/2 cup chopped fresh herbs (thyme, basil, etc.)

- soaked bamboo skewers
- 12 thick slices crusty bread
- snipped chives or chopped parsley

1 *Heat the oven to 325°F / 160°C. Put the garlic and oil in an ovenproof platter and bake for 1 hour until soft. Press the cloves through a sieve to purée them.*

2 *Mix together the marinade ingredients and marinate the mushrooms for at least 2 hours.*

3 *Remove the mushrooms from the marinade. Thread them onto skewers and grill over a medium heat for 5 minutes, basting with the marinade juices. Reduce the rest of the marinade at the side of the grill.*

4 *Grill the slices of bread on both sides and spread with the garlic purée. Top with the grilled mushrooms, reduced marinade, fresh pepper, and chives or parsley.*

❦ **SERVES 6** (TWO TOASTS PER PERSON)

ARTICHOKE SOUP

- 6 large globe artichokes
- 4 tablespoons olive oil
- salt and freshly ground pepper
- 1 clove garlic, minced
- 1 medium onion, chopped
- 5 cups / 1.2 litres chicken stock
- 1 1/2 cups / 300 ml cream
- cayenne pepper, to taste

1 *Cut off the stems and pull off the outer leaves of the artichokes. With a sharp knife, cut around the base to remove the hearts. Toss the hearts with with half of the olive oil and season with salt and plenty of pepper. Marinate for 1 hour.*

2 *Place the hearts on an oiled grill over a low heat and cook for 10 - 15 minutes until browned and tender. Slice the hearts.*

3 *Heat the rest of the olive oil, add the garlic and onion, and cook over a low heat for 10 minutes. Add the artichoke slices. Cover and cook for 10 minutes. Add the chicken stock and simmer for 10 minutes.*

4 *Purée the mixture in a blender or food processor, leaving some texture. Allow the mixture to cool, then stir in the cream and season with cayenne pepper, salt, and pepper. Serve chilled.*

❦ **SERVES 6**

TOMATO SOUP WITH HERBS

2 lbs / 900 g tomatoes
1/2 cup / 100 g butter
2 tablespoons olive oil
2 cloves garlic, minced
3 cups / 700 ml chicken stock
4 tablespoons chopped fresh oregano, basil, or herb of choice
1 cup / 225 ml cream
cayenne pepper, to taste
salt and freshly ground pepper

1 *Grill the tomatoes until the skin begins to char. When cool, peel the tomatoes and remove the seeds.*

2 *Melt the butter over a low heat and add the olive oil. Stir in the garlic and sauté until fragrant. Lower the heat and add the tomatoes. Cook for about 15 minutes, breaking up the tomatoes with a spoon as they soften.*

3 *Add the chicken stock and simmer for 10 minutes. Add the fresh herbs and cream, and season to taste with cayenne pepper, salt, and pepper. Serve hot or at room temperature.*

SERVES 6

PASTA WITH TOMATO, EGGPLANT, AND CREAM SAUCE

1 1/2 lbs / 700 g ripe tomatoes, halved and seeded
1 1/2 lbs / 700 g eggplants (aubergines), cut into 1/2-inch / 1-cm slices
salt and freshly ground pepper
olive oil
3/4 cup / 175 g butter
3 - 4 cloves garlic, minced
1 1/2 cups / 300 ml cream
cayenne pepper
salt and freshly ground pepper
fresh basil, flat-leaved parsley, or oregano
fresh pasta to serve 6

1 *Season the tomato halves and eggplant slices with salt and pepper, and brush with olive oil. Place on an oiled grill over a medium heat and cook until the eggplant slices are golden and the tomatoes are soft (about 5 minutes with the skin side down).*

2 *Melt the butter and sauté the garlic until it just begins to color. Chop and add the tomatoes, and cook over a low heat until a sauce forms. Chop the eggplant slices into bite-size pieces, add them to the tomato mixture, and cook for 5 minutes. Stir in the cream and cook until the mixture begins to thicken. Season to taste. Stir in the torn basil, parsley, or oregano .*

3 *Cook the pasta in boiling, salted water until* al dente. *Drain and add to the tomato and eggplant mixture. Serve hot.*

SERVES 6

SCALLOPS WITH PROSCIUTTO

- juice of 2 lemons and 4 limes
- 8 shallots, sliced
- 2 tablespoons olive oil
- salt and freshly ground pepper
- 24 - 36 fresh scallops without shells
- olive oil
- balsamic, sherry, or red wine vinegar
- 8 oz / 225 g prosciutto (Parma ham), Westphalian ham, or lachs schinken
- 1 cup coarsely torn fresh basil, snipped chives or flat-leaved parsley

1 *Mix together the lemon and lime juice, shallots, oil, salt and pepper. Add the scallops and set aside for 1 hour. Drain the scallops. Reserve the marinade liquor.*

2 *Toss the scallops in a few tablespoons of olive oil. Place on the grill over a medium heat and cook for about 2 minutes on each side, brushing with more olive oil.*

3 *The ham can also be grilled, if desired. Brush with olive oil and grill until it begins to turn golden. Chop or cut into thin strips. If you decide not to grill your ham, just cut it into thin strips.*

4 *Pour the reserved marinade into a small saucepan on the side of the grill. Heat to reduce it, then add vinegar and olive oil to taste to make a warm vinaigrette. Season with salt and pepper, and stir in the fresh herbs.*

5 *Arrange the scallops on individual plates,strew ham over them, and serve with the vinaigrette.*

Scallops are also delicious with Black Bean Sauce (see recipe page 79), in which case you should substitute sesame oil for olive oil.

❦ **SERVES 6**

EGGPLANT AND CHILI SOUP

2 1/2 lbs/ 1.25 kg eggplants (aubergines)
1 medium onion, chopped
5 cloves garlic, chopped
2 - 3 hot fresh chili peppers, coarsely chopped
6 tablespoons olive oil
salt and freshly ground pepper
6 cups / 1.3 litres chicken stock
1 cup / 225 ml cream
snipped chives, to garnish

1 *Grill the eggplants over a medium heat until the skin is blackened. When cool, remove the skin and cut into 1-inch / 2.5-cm cubes.*

2 *Heat the olive oil over a low heat. Add the onion, garlic, and chili, and cook for 5 minutes. Add the eggplant cubes and cook over a low heat for 20 minutes until soft. Season with salt and pepper. Add the chicken stock, cover, and cook for 10 minutes over a medium low heat.*

3 *Purée the mixture in a blender or food processor. Stir in the cream. Reheat (but do not boil) and sprinkle with chives to serve.*

❦ **SERVES 6 TO 8**

CLAMS WITH HERBED BUTTER

6 - 8 clams per person
HERBED BUTTER
3/4 cup / 175 g butter
2 cloves garlic, minced
2 tablespoons lime or lemon juice
grated zest of 1 lime or 1/2 lemon
4 tablespoons fresh oregano, parsley,
or herb of choice
salt and freshly ground pepper

1 *Soak the clams in salted water for about 2 hours to remove the sand. Place on the grill over a medium high heat and cook for about 5 minutes, or until the shells begin to open. Discard any that do not open.*

2 *In a small saucepan on the side of the grill, melt the butter, stir in the remaining ingredients, and season with salt and pepper.*

3 *Serve each person with a plate of clams and a small bowl of herbed butter.*

Clams are also good with Black Bean Sauce (see recipe page 79). Mussels can be grilled in exactly the same way as clams.

❦ **SAUCE SERVES 6**

OYSTERS WITH CAVIAR BUTTER

- 3 dozen fresh oysters
- 4 oz / 125 g red or black caviar
- Rich Mignonette Sauce (see recipe opposite)

1 *Wash the oysters well to remove the sand, then place them on the grill with the flat half of the shell uppermost. Cook over a medium high heat for about 4 minutes, or until the shells just begin to open. Remove from the heat. Using an oyster knife, finish opening the shells, discarding the flat top shells.*

2 *Arrange the oysters on a serving platter or on bed of heated rock salt. Drop a teaspoon of Rich Mignonette Sauce into each oyster, and top with a sprinkling of caviar.*

❦ **SERVES 6**

OYSTERS WITH MIGNONETTE SAUCE

- 3 dozen fresh oysters in their shells

MIGNONETTE SAUCE

- 4 shallots
- 1 cup / 225 ml dry white wine
- 4 - 8 tablespoons sherry vinegar or champagne vinegar
- freshly ground pepper

1 *Wash the oysters well to remove the sand. Place on the grill over a medium high heat, with the flattest half of the shell uppermost. Grill for 4 minutes, or until the shells begin to open. Do not flip the oysters over during cooking.*

2 *To make the Mignonette Sauce., mix together the shallots, wine, vinegar, and pepper, and boil until the liquid is reduced to 4 tablespoons. Keep the sauce warm on the side of the grill.*

3 *Remove the oysters from the grill and finish opening them - use an oyster knife or a knife with short blade and finger guard. Discard the flat top shells. Arrange on individual serving plates - or on a bed of heated rock salt - and serve with small bowls of sauce.*

A richer version of Mignonette Sauce would be 4 minced shallots, 1 cup / 225 ml red or dry white wine, 1 teaspoon salt, 2 - 4 tablespoons sherry vinegar, and 1 cup / 225 g butter cut into small pieces. Combine the shallots, wine, salt, and vinegar, and boil until the liquid is reduced to 4 tablespoons. Then beat in the butter.

❦ **SERVES 6 TO 8**

SHRIMP AND ARTICHOKE SOUP

2 lbs / 900 g unpeeled shrimps or prawns, with heads

SHRIMP MARINADE

3 lemons (juice of all 3 and grated zest of 1)

2 fresh chili peppers, chopped

1 teaspoon coarse salt

6 globe artichokes, trimmed down to the heart

3 tablespoons olive oil

salt and freshly ground pepper

STOCK

1/2 cup / 100 g butter

2 tablespoons olive oil

3 cloves garlic, halved

1 bottle dry white wine

6 cups / 1.35 litres water

6 peppercorns

1 teaspoon salt

olive oil

Zhoug Relish (see recipe page 23) or 1 cup fresh coriander - optional

1 *Remove the shrimp heads and reserve. Mix together the marinade ingredients and stir in the shrimps. Marinate for at least 4 hours or overnight.*

2 *Marinate the artichoke hearts in olive oil seasoned with salt and pepper.*

3 *To make the stock, melt the butter and add the olive oil, and sauté the shrimp heads and garlic halves for about 10 minutes, stirring often until you have a rich stock base. Add the wine, water, and peppercorns, and salt to taste, bring to a boil, and simmer over a low heat for about 30 minutes until the liquid has reduced to half. Strain, reserving the liquid but discarding the contents of the strainer.*

4 *Drain the artichoke hearts and place them on an oiled grill. Cook over a medium heat for about 15 minutes, occasionally basting with olive oil, until tender and golden. Cut into slices 1/4-inch / 0.5 cm thick.*

5 *Remove the shrimps from the marinade. Strain the marinade and set aside. Toss the shrimps in a little olive oil, thread them onto skewers, and cook over a medium heat for about 1 1/2 minutes on each side.*

6 *Reheat the shrimp stock and season it to taste with the reserved shrimp marinade and a little Zhoug Relish or fresh coriander, if liked. Add the artichoke slices and peeled shrimps just before serving.*

This soup can be prepared without the artichokes, if preferred. The shrimps and the artichokes can also be prepared in advance.

❦ **SERVES 6 TO 8**

MUSSELS WITH CHILI VINAIGRETTE

1 - 2 fresh chili peppers, seeded and thinly sliced
1 cup chopped fresh coriander or flat-leaved parsley
3/4 cup / 175 ml Basic Vinaigrette (see recipe page 48) or Lemon Mustard Dressing (see recipe page 54)
salt and freshly ground pepper
48 large fresh mussels, soaked in salted water

1 *Mix the chili peppers and herbs with the vinaigrette, and add salt and pepper to taste.*

2 *Place the mussels directly on the grill over a medium heat and cook until they begin to open (discard those that do not open).*

3 *Remove one shell from each mussel. Arrange on a serving platter and spoon the vinaigrette over them.*

❦ **SERVES 6**

CALAMARI WITH SOY AND SAKE

3/4 cup / 175 ml sake
3/4 cup / 175 g sugar
3/4 cup / 175 ml soy sauce
1 1/2 lbs / 700 g calamari (baby squid), cleaned, with tentacles
soaked bamboo skewers - optional

1 *Mix together the sake, sugar, and soy sauce. Add the calamari and toss well. Marinate for 1 hour.*

2 *Drain the calamari and reserve the marinade. Place the calamari on the grill (skewered for easier turning if you wish) and cook over a high heat for 20 seconds on each side (longer if the calamari are fairly large), basting with the marinade. Reduce the rest of the marinade to thicken it and pour over the calamari to serve.*

❦ **SERVES 6**

SEVICHE WITH SAUSAGES

2 cups / 450 ml fresh lemon juice
1/2 tablespoons coarse salt
2 lbs / 900 g red snapper (or grouper) fillet
3 tablespoons olive oil
2 cups chopped onion
3/4 cup chopped green olives
2 - 3 tablespoons Worcestershire sauce
1 teaspoon tabasco sauce, or to taste
2 - 3 hot fresh green chili peppers,
thinly sliced
3 firm tomatoes, seeded and chopped
4 tablespoons chopped flat-leaved parsley
or coriander
1 lb / 450 g hot Polish, Cajun, or other hot,
spicy sausages

1 *Mix together the lemon juice and salt and pour over the fish. Turn the fish to make sure that all of it comes into contact with the marinade. Marinate for 4 - 6 hours.*

2 *Remove the fish from the marinade and reserve the juices. Brush both sides of the fillet with olive oil and place on the grill over a high heat. Cook very quickly (1 - 2 minutes per side) so that the fillet is slightly charred on the outside, but very rare inside.*

3 *Cut the fish into 1 1/2-inch / 4-cm chunks and place in a bowl with the chopped onion, olives, Worcestershire and tabasco sauce, chili peppers, and tomatoes. Add 1/2 cup of the reserved lemon juice marinade and toss well. Refrigerate overnight. The next day, add the parsley or coriander. Adjust the seasoning and add more of the lemon juice marinade if necessary.*

4 *With the sharp point of a small knife, prick the sausages all over and grill over a low heat until cooked and well browned. Arrange on a serving platter with the fish.*

❦ **SERVES 6**

GOOSE LIVER SALAD

BASIC VINAIGRETTE

- 6 tablespoons sherry vinegar
- 2 cloves garlic, minced
- 1 tablespoon Dijon mustard
- 1/2 cup / 100 ml olive oil
- salt and freshly ground pepper

- 1 lb / 450 g goose liver or foie gras, cut into 1-inch / 2.5-cm cubes
- olive oil seasoned with salt and pepper
- 9 cups torn mixed lettuces
- soaked bamboo skewers
- fresh chives, snipped

1 *Prepare the vinaigrette - just beat together all the ingredients, with salt and pepper to taste.*

2 *Thread the cubes of goose liver onto skewers and lightly season with salt and pepper. Place on an oiled grill over a low heat and cook for 1 - 2 minutes, turning the skewers once or twice.*

3 *Place the lettuces in a bowl, toss with an amount of vinaigrette to taste, add the goose liver pieces, and toss again. Add more salt and pepper if desired, and garnish with chives.*

❦ **SERVES 6 TO 8**

GRILLED LETTUCES WITH FETA CHEESE

- 1/2 cup / 100 ml olive oil
- coarse salt and freshly ground pepper
- 12 baby lettuces or 1/2 medium lettuce per person
- 1 1/4 lbs / 600 g feta cheese
- 3 mangoes, peaches, or nectarines, peeled and sliced
- lemon wedges

1 *Spoon the olive oil into a platter and season well with salt and pepper. Cut the lettuces in half, if necessary, and roll them in the oil, coating them well.*

2 *Place the lettuce halves on the grill, cut side down to start with. Cook over a medium low heat for about 4 minutes (longer if the lettuces are large), basting with olive oil and turning ocasionally.*

3 *Place the lettuce halves on a serving platter or on individual plates. Add portions of feta cheese, slices of fruit, and lemon wedges. Drizzle with a little olive oil.*

The fruit can be grilled too. Place slices on the grill, brush with olive oil, and cook until golden brown.

❦ **SERVES 6 TO 8**

Salads

LET US SING A BALLAD

TO THE SALAD

WHICH IS HASTY

AND EVEN TASTY.

Ogden Nash

American poet

(1902 - 1971)

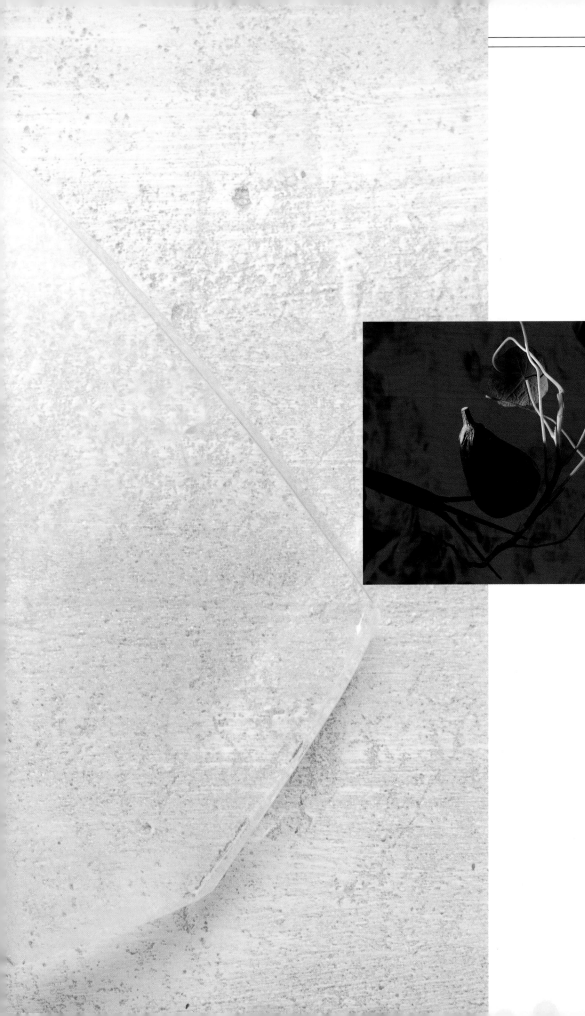

Salads

There is no more flexible item on a menu than a salad. Made from a nearly infinite variety of greenery, vegetables, herbs, flowers, eggs, cheese, meat, poultry, and fish seasoned with oil, vinegar, salt, pepper, and a host of other flavorings, salads can be served as main or first courses, as accompaniments to main courses or, in the French style, to refresh the palate after the main course.

❦ *It goes without saying that the freshest produce and the finest quality olive or nut oils are critical to producing a good salad. As for vinegar, don't be afraid to experiment (one of my own favorites is sherry vinegar).*

❦ *As you have probably noticed, the taste of a salad changes with the temperature at which it is eaten. Salads can be served chilled, at room temperature, or mixed with warm ingredients.*

❦ *But bear in mind that texture is as important as taste in a salad. A soggy salad is an affront to creation. There should be just enough dressing to lightly coat the ingredients.*

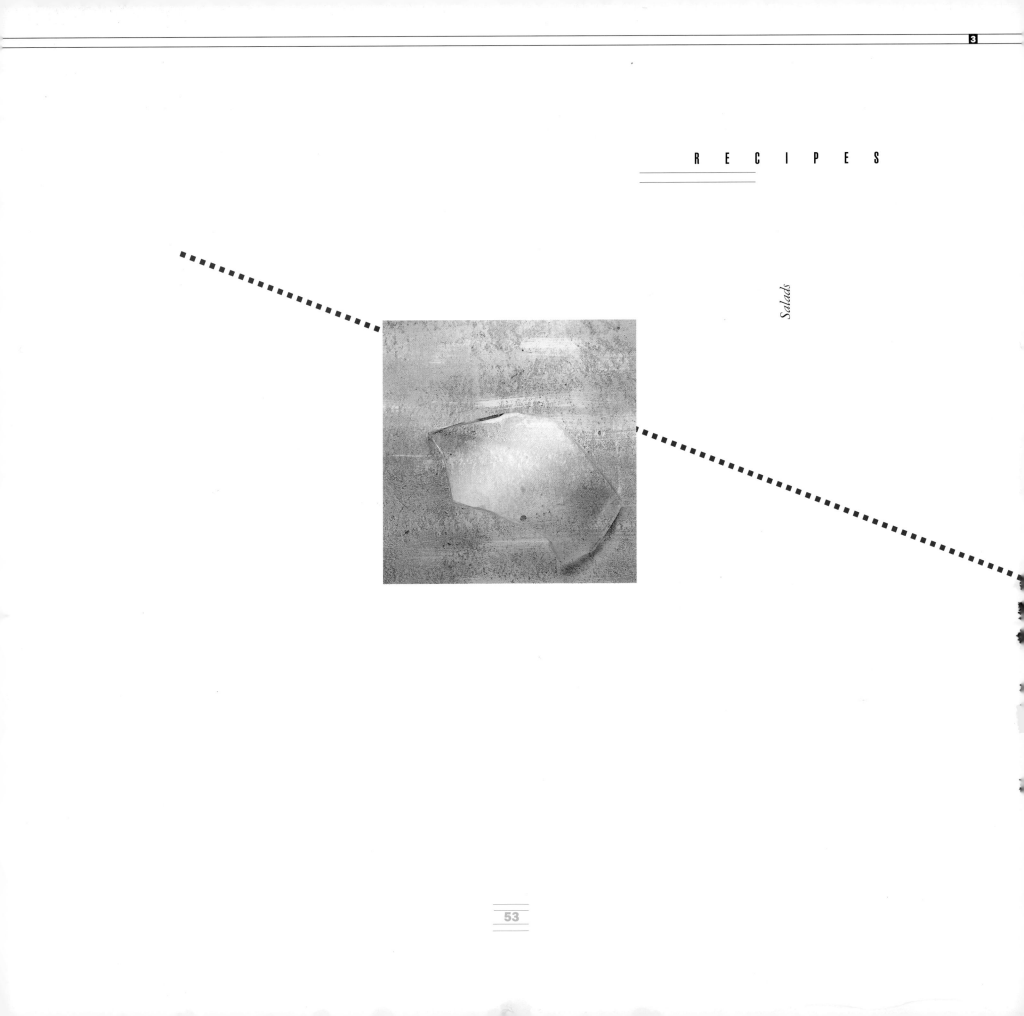

RECIPES

Salads

GRILLED VEGETABLE AND PASTA SALAD

- 4 large ripe tomatoes, halved and seeded
- 4 fresh artichoke hearts, trimmed
- 1 lb / 450 g Japanese eggplants (aubergines), cut lengthwise into slices 1/2 inch / 1 cm thick
- 2 red onions, peeled and cut into slices 1/2 inch/ 1 cm thick
- olive oil
- 1 cup chopped fresh basil or oregano
- 1/2 cup chopped fresh flat parsley
- salt and freshly ground pepper
- Lemon Mustard Dressing (see recipe below right) or Basic Vinaigrette (see recipe page 48)
- 1 lb / 450 g fresh pasta, cooked *al dente*

1 *Brush the vegetables with plenty of olive oil, and season with salt and pepper. Grill the tomatoes first, over a medium heat, skin side down, until brown and tender. Then grill the eggplant and onion slices. Put the artichokes on the side of the grill where it is cooler, and cook for 10 - 15 minutes until crisp, tender and golden brown. Turn and baste frequently with olive oil. When all the vegetables are cooked, allow them to cool slightly.*

2 *Chop the vegetables into uneven, bite-size pieces. Toss the pasta in a little olive oil and add the chopped vegetables. Toss with Lemon Mustard Dressing or Basic Vinaigrette to taste, adding the herbs and more salt and pepper if desired. Marinate for several hours or overnight. Taste before serving to see if you need to add more dresssing or seasoning.*

❦ **SERVES 4** AS A MAIN COURSE

MINT HONEY SAUCE

A FRAGRANT AND EXOTIC MARINADE FOR CHICKEN OR LAMB

- 1 1/2 cups fresh mint leaves
- 1 1/2 cups fresh coriander leaves
- 6 cloves garlic, minced
- 6 slices peeled fresh ginger, minced
- 2 fresh green chili peppers, seeded and minced
- 1 teaspoon salt
- juice of 3 lemons
- 6 tablespoons soy sauce
- 6 tablespoons vegetable oil, part sesame if possible
- 3 tablespoons honey
- 2 tablespoons wine vinegar

1 *Simply mix all the ingredients together and beat well. Use immediately, or store in a sealed jar in the refrigerator.*

❦ **MAKES ABOUT 2 CUPS / 600 ml**

LEMON MUSTARD DRESSING

EXCELLENT WITH SALAD VEGETABLES, CHICKEN, OR FISH

- 6 cloves garlic, crushed
- 1/2 teaspoon salt
- 3 - 4 tablespoons Dijon mustard
- 4 tablespoons fresh lemon juice
- 6 tablespoons olive oil, to taste
- 1 1/2 teaspoons freshly ground pepper
- cayenne pepper, to taste

1 *Combine all the ingredients and beat well. Use immediately, or put in a well sealed jar and store in the refrigerator for a day or two.*

❦ **MAKES 1 1/2 CUPS / 325 ml**

CHICKEN SALAD WITH MUSTARD AND PARMESAN DRESSING

6 boneless chicken breasts
Lemon Mustard Marinade (see recipe page 93)

MUSTARD AND PARMESAN DRESSING
2 eggs
1 teaspoon salt
4 - 6 tablespoons Dijon mustard
6 tablespoons fresh lemon juice
2 - 3 teaspoons Worcestershire sauce
1 cup / 225 ml vegetable or olive oil
2 tablespoons fresh thyme leaves
4 tablespoons grated Parmesan cheese

12 cups torn mixed lettuces
4 - 6 scallions (green or spring onions), sliced
1 cup fresh peas, shelled and uncooked - optional
1/2 cup ripe (black) olives, pitted and sliced
2 large avocadoes, peeled, pitted and cut into chunks
tomato wedges to garnish

1 *Marinate the chicken breasts in the Lemon Mustard Marinade for at least 4 hours or overnight.*

2 *Prepare the Mustard and Parmesan Dressing, and allow to stand for at least 2 hours.*

3 *In a large bowl, combine all the salad ingredients.*

4 *Remove the chicken breasts from the marinade and reserve the marinade. Place the chicken on the grill over a medium heat, and cook for 3 minutes on each side, basting occasionally with the marinade.*

5 *Pour the dressing over the vegetables and toss well. Serve on individual plates, with the chicken portions on top.*

❦ **SERVES 6** AS A MAIN COURSE

SALMON AND SPINACH SALAD

1 1/2 tablespoons rock salt
2 1/2 tablespoons sugar
2 lbs / 900 g salmon fillet
olive oil

DRESSING

3 - 4 shallots, chopped
1/2 cup / 100 ml red wine vinegar or sherry vinegar
2/3 cup / 150 ml olive oil, or to taste
grated zest of 1 lemon
1 lb / 450 g tomatoes, skinned, seeded and diced
1 red onion, halved, thinly sliced, and separated into rings
salt and freshly ground pepper

10 cups young spinach leaves, torn

1 *Combine the salt and sugar and rub into the salmon. Place in an oiled dish and cover with a damp cloth. Refrigerate overnight.*

2 *Combine the ingredients for the dressing, adding salt and pepper to taste. Set aside for 1 hour.*

3 *Wipe the salmon with a damp cloth, brush with olive oil, and season with pepper. Place on an oiled grill over a high heat. Cook for 3 - 4 minutes on each side. When cool, break the salmon into large flakes, add the spinach, and toss with dressing to taste.*

❦ **SERVES 6** AS A MAIN COURSE

CHINESE CHICKEN SALAD

2 cups Mint Honey Sauce (see recipe page 54)
4 boneless chicken breasts, with skin
3 cups torn fresh spinach
2 cups torn lettuce
1 cup grated carrot
1 cup fresh peas, shelled
6 scallions (spring onions), cut into 1-inch /2.5-cm pieces
1 cup chopped celery
2 cups bean sprouts
1 cup toasted almonds, coarsely chopped

1 *Prepare the Mint Honey Sauce. Use half the quantity to marinate the chicken breasts, making sure you rub some of sauce under the skin. Marinate for 4 hours or overnight.*

2 *Combine the rest of the ingredients in a large bowl.*

3 *Remove the chicken from the marinade and reserve the marinade. Place the chicken on an oiled grill over a medium heat and cook for about 8 minutes, turning once and basting well with the marinade.*

4 *Pour the remaining Mint Honey Sauce over the salad ingredients and toss well. Serve on individual plates, with the sliced chicken on top.*

❦ **SERVES 6** AS A MAIN COURSE

STEAK SALAD

MARINADE
6 tablespoons balsamic, sherry, red wine, or herbed vinegar
6 tablespoons olive oil
4 cloves garlic, minced
6 sirloin or New York steaks weighing 6 oz / 200 g each
2 large red onions, peeled and cut into 1/2 - inch / 1 - cm slices
olive oil

SPICE RUB
1 cup chopped fresh thyme or oregano
1 teaspoon coarse salt
1 - 2 teaspoons coarsely ground pepper

Basic Vinaigrette (see recipe page 48)
2 bunches arugula or curly endive
8 cups torn romaine (cos) lettuce
6 scallions (green or spring onions), chopped
2 tomatoes, cut into wedges
salt and pepper

1 *Combine the marinade ingredients and pour over the steaks and onions slices. Marinate for 3 hours or overnight.*

2 *Mix together the ingredients for the spice rub. Remove the steaks and onion slices from the marinade. Brush steak and onions with olive oil and season the meat with the spice rub.*

3 *Place meat and onions on the grill over a medium heat. Cook the steaks for about 4 minutes on each side (the meat should be rare inside) and the onion slices until crisp, tender, and nicely browned. Let the meat rest for 10 minutes before slicing.*

4 *Cut the steaks diagonally across the grain into slices 1/2 inch / 1 cm thick. Halve and separate the onion slices. Toss both steak and onion slices in vinaigrette to taste.*

5 *Put the arugula, lettuce, tomatoes, and scallions in a bowl and toss with vinaigrette to taste. Season with salt and pepper. Top with the steak and onion slices.*

Grilled shitake or oyster mushrooms make a delicious addition to this recipe.

❦ **SERVES 6** AS A MAIN COURSE

SEAFOOD SALAD

MARINADE

- juice of 2 lemons and grated zest of 1
- juice of 4 limes and grated zest of 2
- 2 - 4 fresh chili peppers, seeded and thinly sliced
- 8 shallots, peeled and thinly sliced
- 1 teaspoon coarse salt
- freshly ground pepper
- 4 tablespoons olive oil

- 1 lb / 450 g prawns in their shells, split in half
- 1 lb / 450 g scallops without shells
- 1 lb / 450 g calamari (baby squid), cleaned, with tentacles
- soaked bamboo skewers
- olive oil
- Lemon Mustard Dressing (see recipe page 54)
- 6 - 8 scallions (green or spring onions), finely chopped
- 1 cup chopped fresh basil, coriander or flat-leaved parsley, or a combination of fresh mint and coriander
- 20 ripe (black) oil-cured olives, pitted - optional
- salt and freshly ground pepper
- 1 1/2 cups / 350 g long grain rice, cooked **OR** 8 - 12 oz / 225 - 350 g pasta, cooked *al dente* - optional

1 *Mix together all the marinade ingredients and pour over the prawns, scallops, and calamari. Marinate for 3 - 4 hours. Drain the seafood and reserve the marinade. Toss the seafood in olive oil.*

2 *Thread the seafood onto skewers. Place on the grill over a high heat. Cook the calamari about 1 minute on each side, and the scallops and prawns 2 minutes on each side. Turn and baste occasionally with olive oil.*

3 *Shell the prawns and cut the calamari into rings. Halve the scallops if they are large.*

4 *Toss the seafood with Lemon Mustard Dressing to taste and add the scallions, herbs, and olives (optional). Season with salt and pepper. Marinate for 2 hours or overnight, adding the rice or pasta (if using) just before serving.*

Instead of Lemon Mustard Dressing, you could use some of the reserved marinade mixed with balsamic or sherry vinegar and olive oil. Fine strips of prosciutto would also make an excellent addition.

❦ **SERVES 6** AS A MAIN COURSE

CALAMARI AND ARUGULA SALAD

- 3 tablespoons olive oil
- salt and freshly ground pepper
- 2 teaspoons Zhoug Relish (see recipe page 23) - optional
- 2 lbs / 900 g fresh calamari (baby squid), cleaned, with tentacles
- soaked bamboo skewers
- Lemon Mustard Dressing (see recipe page 54)
- 6 scallions (green or spring onions), sliced
- 8 oz / 225 g prosciutto (Parma ham) or lachs schinken - optional
- arugula or curly endive
- 1 lettuce - optional

1 *Season the olive oil with salt and pepper, and with Zhoug Relish if liked. Marinate the calamari bodies and tentacles in this mixture for 1 hour. Remove them from the marinade and reserve the marinade. Thread the bodies and tentacles separately onto soaked bamboo skewers.*

2 *Place the skewers on an oiled grill over a high heat. Cook for 1 1/2 minutes on both sides, basting with the reserved marinade - the bodies will turn white and opaque and the tentacles will turn pink and spotted. Allow the skewers to cool slightly.*

3 *Mix together all the ingredients for the Lemon Mustard Dressing.*

4 *Slice the calamari bodies into thin rings, leaving the tentacles whole. Add the sliced scallions and toss well with Lemon Mustard Dressing to taste. Marinate in the refrigerator for 1 or 2 days. Just before serving, add the prosciutto (optional), cut into fine strips.*

5 *Serve on a bed of arugula or lettuce, or toss well with arugula or lettuce before serving.*

SERVES 8 TO 10 AS A STARTER

TUNA SALAD

- 2 lbs / 900 g fresh tuna fillet
- 1 cup / 225 ml olive oil
- 6 tablespoons lemon juice
- grated zest of 1 lemon
- 6 - 8 cloves garlic, minced
- 20 ripe (black) olives, pitted
- 5 tablespoons chopped fresh oregano or basil
- 5 tablespoons chopped shallot
- 6 scallions (green or spring onions), thinly sliced
- 6 tomatoes, cut into wedges
- 12 cups torn mixed lettuce, arugala, or curly endive
- salt and freshly ground pepper
- extra lemon juice

1 *Mix together 6 tablespoons of the olive oil, the lemon juice and zest, and half the garlic. Pour over the tuna, then turn the tuna so that both sides are well coated. Marinate for at least 4 hours, turning once.*

2 *Place the tuna on an oiled grill over a high heat and cook for about 5 minutes, turning once. Do not overcook - the outside of the fish should be charred and the inside rare. Remove from the grill and allow to rest for a few minutes. Cut into slices 1 inch / 2.5 cm thick.*

3 *In a large bowl, combine the rest of the olive oil with the olives, herbs, shallot, scallions, and tomatoes. Add the tuna slices. Add salt and extra lemon juice to taste, and a few grinds of pepper. Allow to stand for at least 2 hours. Put the lettuce on individual plates and serve the tuna salad on top.*

❦ **SERVES 6** AS A MAIN COURSE.

OKRA, CORN, AND BASIL SALAD

- 3 tablespoons olive oil
- salt and freshly ground pepper
- 1 lb / small fresh okra, with 1/4 inch / 0.5 cm of stem attached
- soaked bamboo skewers
- 2 cobs sweetcorn, without leaves

DRESSING

- 4 tablespoons olive oil
- 2 - 4 tablespoons fresh lemon juice
- 2 tablespoons grated zest of lemon - optional
- 1 teaspoon coarse salt
- 1/2 - 1 cup fresh basil leaves, torn
- tabasco sauce, to taste

1 *Mix together the 3 tablespoons of olive oil with salt and pepper, pour over the okra, and toss well. Marinate for at least 1 hour.*

2 *Thread the okra onto skewers. Place the skewers and the corn cobs on an oiled grill over a medium heat. Cook, basting with the oil in which the okra were marinated, until crisp and golden.*

3 *Mix together all the dressing ingredients. With a sharp knife, remove the corn kernels from the cobs, add the grilled okra, and toss well with the dressing. Allow to stand for at least 1 hour before serving.*

❦ **SERVES 4** AS A STARTER OR SIDE SALAD

RUSTIC SALAD

- 1/2 cup / 100 ml olive oil
- salt and freshly ground pepper
- 4 large ripe tomatoes, halved and seeded - optional
- 4 baby lettuces, endive, or radicchio, halved
- 10 shallots, peeled and soaked in warm water for 15 minutes
- 4 cobs sweetcorn, without leaves
- 8 Japanese eggplants (aubergines), cut lengthwise into slices 1/2 inch / 1 cm thick
- 8 small potatoes
- fresh herbs (basil, rosemary, oregano, or parsley)
- Lemon Mustard Dressing (see recipe page 54) or Basic Vinaigrette (see recipe page 48)

1 *Season the olive oil with salt and pepper and use it brush the vegetables - tomatoes (if using), lettuces, shallots, sweetcorn, eggplants, and potatoes. Marinate for 1 - 2 hours.*

2 *Place the vegetables on an oiled grill over a medium heat. Cook, basting with olive oil from the marinade, until they are golden and tender. The potatoes will take the longest. Remove all the vegetables from the grill and allow them to cool slightly. Cut the kernels from the corn cobs and cut the rest of the vegetables into chunks. Toss with the fresh herb of your choice. Add Lemon Mustard Dressing or Basic Vinaigrette to taste, toss well, and allow to stand for a few hours before serving.*

❦ **SERVES 6 TO 8** AS A SIDE SALAD

ARTICHOKE, FENNEL, AND POTATO SALAD

- 4 large globe artichokes
- 4 bulbs fennel
- 12 small potatoes
- 2 large red onions
- olive oil
- salt and freshly ground pepper
- Lemon Mustard Dressing (see recipe page 54) or Basic Vinaigrette (see recipe page 48)

1 *Trim the artichokes down to the heart. Trim off the outer leaves of the fennel and cut the bulbs in half lengthwise. Thoroughly scrub the potatoes and dry them with a cloth. Peel the onions and cut them into slices 1/2 inch / 1 cm thick. Marinate in seasoned olive oil for at least 1 hour.*

2 *Place all the vegetables on an oiled grill over a medium heat, starting with the potatoes. Cook until crisp, tender, and golden brown - the potatoes will take the longest.*

3 *Prepare the Lemon Mustard Dressing or Basic Vinaigrette.*

4 *While the vegetables are still warm, cut them into smaller chunks or slices and pour a little dressing over them. Allow to stand for at least 2 hours. Before serving, add more dressing to taste and check the seasoning.*

❦ **SERVES 6** AS A STARTER OR SIDE SALAD

Fish & Seafood

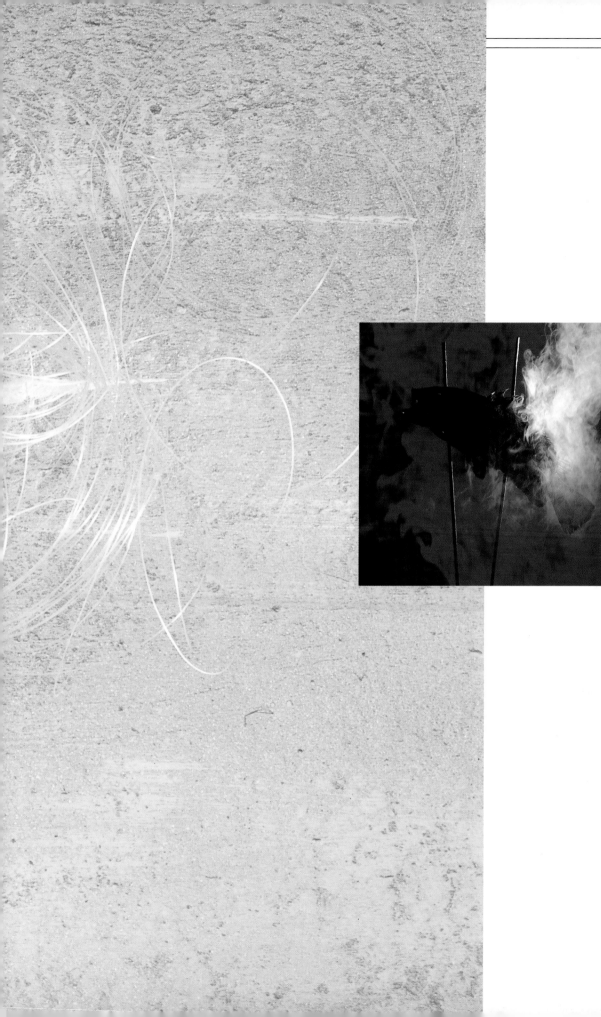

It was not, I think, until my first visit to the Mediterranean that I began to appreciate the beauty of red mullet, bass, or sardines brought straight from the sea to the grill and served crackling and golden with no garnish but a lemon. Since those days I have nearly always preferred grilled sole, trout, salmon, mullet, herring, or mackerel to any subtle concoction of sole, lobster, or turbot with cream, wine, or mushrooms.

Elizabeth David

English cookery writer

(b. 1913)

CHAPTER FOUR

Fish & Seafood

Grilling is one of the best and easiest methods of cooking fish, and the best fish for grilling are firm-fleshed, oily ones such as tuna, swordfish, salmon, grouper, snapper, and mackerel. In my opinion, whole fish should be served with the head and tail on.

❦ *Most fish should be placed on a grill set about 4 inches (10 cm) above a high or medium high heat. A hinged wire basket makes for easier turning, especially of small fish, scallops, calamari, and prawns. Most whole fish take about 8 minutes of cooking for every inch (2.5 cm) of thickness.*

❦ *Fish is often said to be cooked when it "flakes easily at the touch of a fork," but my own feeling is that a fish that flakes easily is a fish that has been overcooked. To test a fish for doneness, stick a knife tip or bamboo skewer into the thickest part of it. When done, the flesh should look opaque and moist, not semi-transparent or fibrous. An overcooked fish tastes dry, and overcooked shellfish have a remarkable resemblance to rubber.*

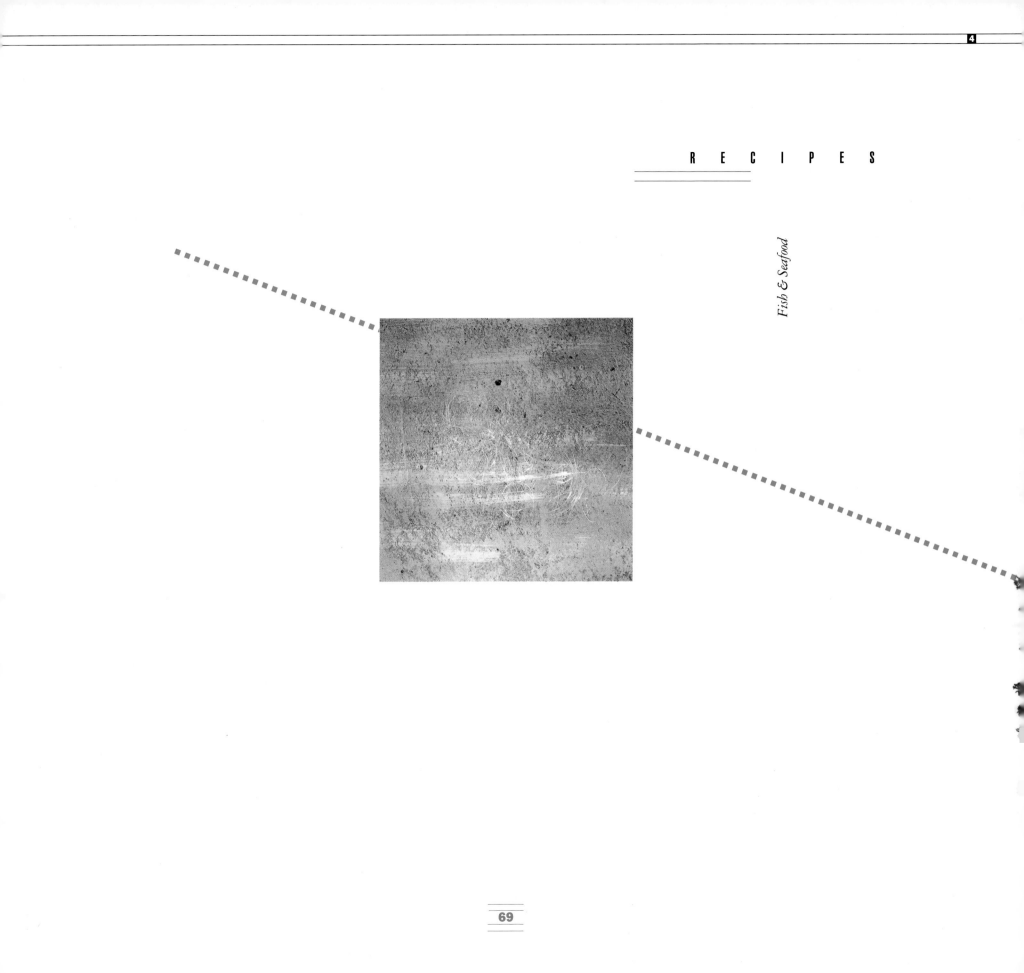

RECIPES

Fish & Seafood

SEA BASS WITH CHILI AND CORIANDER BUTTER

1 whole sea bass or several smaller fish, weighing 4 - 5 lbs / 1.8 - 2.25 kg with head and tail
juice of 2 lemons
2 teaspoons coarse salt
4 cloves garlic, minced
2 hot chili peppers, chopped

CHILI AND CORIANDER BUTTER

2 shallots, coarsely chopped
1 - 2 fresh chili peppers, seeded and coarsely chopped
1 1/2 cups fresh coriander, coarsely chopped
2 tablespoons fresh lime or lemon juice
2 teaspoons grated zest of lemon or lime
1/2 teaspoon salt
freshly ground pepper
1 cup / 225 g melted butter

1 *Make diagonal slits in both sides of the fish. Combine the lemon juice, salt, garlic and chili peppers, and rub them into the fish, inside and out. Cover and set aside for at least 2 hours. Blend together all the Chili and Coriander Butter ingredients, adding the butter last.*

2 *Place the fish on an oiled grill over a medium high heat and brush well with the Chili and Coriander Butter. Cook for 10 - 12 minutes on each side. Serve with the rest of the butter mixture.*

❦ **SERVES 6 TO 8**

STRIPED BASS WITH ZHOUG SAUCE

1 whole striped bass (about 4 lbs / 1.8 kg) or several smaller fish, with head and tail

ZHOUG SAUCE

1 cup / 225 ml olive oil
1/3 - 2/3 cup/ 75 - 150 ml fresh lemon juice
1 - 3 tablespoons Zhoug Relish (see recipe page 23)
salt and freshly ground pepper

2 tomatoes, finely chopped

1 *Split the fish open like a book. Combine all the sauce ingredients and pour half over the fish. Marinate for 1 hour.*

2 *Remove the fish from the sauce and reserve the sauce. Place the fish on an oiled grill over a medium heat. Cook for 5 - 7 minutes on both sides, basting frequently with the reserved sauce.*

3 *Add the chopped tomatoes to the rest of the sauce, heat it on the side of the grill, and pour over the fish to serve.*

❦ **SERVES 6**

WHOLE FISH WITH FRESH HERBS

- 3 cloves garlic, minced
- 2 cups fresh herbs (dill, basil, mint, rosemary, flat-leaved parsley, and coriander, or a mixture of herbs to taste)
- 1 - 2 teaspoons coarse salt
- freshly ground pepper
- 1 whole firm-fleshed fish, weighing 5 lbs / 2.2 kg, or two smaller fish, cleaned, with head and tail
- 6 tablespoons olive oil
- lemon wedges

1 *Pound together the garlic, herbs, salt, and pepper, and blend in the olive oil. Make several shallow slashes in the sides of the fish. Rub the garlic and herb mixture into the slashes and into the inside of the fish. Set aside for at least 1 hour.*

2 *Place the fish on an oiled grill over a medium heat. Cook for 4 - 10 minutes on each side (depending on size), basting occasionally with olive oil. Serve with lemon wedges.*

❦ **SERVES 6**

CURED SALMON STEAKS WITH HERBS

- 1 1/2 tablespoons coarse salt
- 3 tablespoons sugar
- 6 salmon steaks, weighing 7 oz / 200 g each
- sprigs of fresh dill, basil, or tarragon
- olive oil
- Herb and Lemon Salsa (see recipe opposite page) - optional

1 *Sprinkle the salt and sugar over the salmon steaks. Strew the bottom of a platter with the herbs and place the steaks on top. Cover with a damp cloth and refrigerate for 24 hours.*

2 *Before grilling, wipe the steaks with a damp cloth to remove any salt, sugar, or herbs adhering to them. Lightly brush the steaks with olive oil. Place on an oiled grill over a medium high heat and cook for 2 - 3 minutes on each side. The fish should be cooked on the outside but semi-rare inside. Serve with Herb and Lemon Salsa, if desired.*

❦ **SERVES 6**

FISH STEAKS WITH HERB AND LEMON SALSA

6 fish steaks about 1/2 inch / 1 cm thick, weighing 6 - 8 oz / 175 - 225 g each
coarse salt
olive oil
freshly ground pepper

HERB AND LEMON SALSA

1 lb / 450 g tomatoes, seeded and diced
2 - 3 cloves garlic, minced
1 cup chopped fresh basil, coriander, or other herb
8 tablespoons olive oil
2 tablespoons wine, sherry, or balsamic vinegar
grated zest of 1 lemon
3 tablespoons snipped chives
1 - 2 hot chili peppers, seeded and minced - optional

olive oil

1 *Rub a little salt into the fish steaks and set aside for 1 hour. Brush with olive oil and add a grind or two of pepper.*

2 *Combine all the salsa ingredients and set aside for 1 hour to allow all the flavors to blend.*

3 *Place the fish steaks on an oiled grill over a medium high heat. Cook for about 4 minutes on each side, basting occasionally with olive oil. Serve with the salsa.*

❦ **SERVES 6**

GRILLED RED SNAPPER

1 whole red snapper, weighing 5 lbs / 2.2 kg, with head, or 2 smaller fish
2 tablespoons salt
juice of 2 lemons
olive oil

1 *Make diagonal slits in the fish. Rub in the salt and lemon juice, and allow to stand for at least 2 hours.*

2 *Brush the fish with olive oil and place on the grill over a medium low heat. Cook for about 10 minutes on both sides, basting occasionally with olive oil.*

This is the simplest and tastiest way of cooking fish. It can be served with lemon wedges, or with Herb and Lemon Salsa (see recipe opposite), Chili and Coriander Butter (see recipe page 70), or Zhoug Sauce (see recipe page 70).

❦ **SERVES 6**

WHOLE FISH WITH CORIANDER VINAIGRETTE

CORIANDER VINAIGRETTE

- 1 1/2 cups chopped fresh coriander (or a mixture of coriander and mint)
- 3 - 4 cloves garlic, minced
- 2 - 3 tablespoons wine vinegar
- juice and grated zest of 1 lemon or lime
- 1 tablespoon paprika
- 1 tablespoon cumin
- 1 teaspoon red chili pepper flakes, crushed
- coarse salt
- cayenne pepper
- 4 tablespoons olive oil

- 1 whole fish weighing 5 lbs / 2.2 kg (snapper, grouper, yellowtail, etc.) or several smaller fish

1 *Combine all the vinaigrette ingredients. Make slits in both sides of the fish or split it open. Pour the vinaigrette over the fish and marinate for 2 hours.*

2 *Remove the fish from the vinaigrette and reserve the vinaigrette. Place the fish on an oiled grill over a medium heat. Cook for 4 - 10 minutes on both sides (depending on size), brushing frequently with the reserved vinaigrette or with olive oil. Heat the remaining vinaigrette at the side of the grill to reduce it a little and pour over the fish to serve.*

❦ **SERVES 6**

TUNA STEAKS WITH ANCHOVY AND OLIVE SAUCE

- 6 tuna steaks 1/2 - 3/4 inch / 1 - 2 cm thick, weighing 8 - 10 oz / 225 - 300 g each
- freshly ground pepper
- 3 tablespoons olive oil

ANCHOVY AND OLIVE SAUCE

- 2 tablespoons chopped shallot
- 2 teaspoons chopped garlic
- 2 cups chopped fresh basil or flat parsley
- 3 - 4 anchovy fillets
- 1 cup ripe (black) olives, pitted
- 4 tablespoons lemon juice
- cayenne pepper
- freshly ground pepper
- 1 cup / 225 g butter, cut into small pieces

1 *Sprinkle the tuna steaks with pepper and coat them with olive oil. Marinate for 2 - 3 hours.*

2 *Put all the sauce ingredients except the butter in a food processer and blend to a coarse paste. Add the butter and reblend.*

3 *Just before grilling, sprinkle the tuna steaks with a little salt. Grill over a medium high heat, basting with the Anchovy and Olive Sauce. Allow 3 minutes for each side (tuna should always be charred outside and very rare inside). Spoon 2 tablespoons of sauce over each steak to serve.*

❦ **SERVES 6**

SEAFOOD PAELLA

2 lbs / 900 g large prawns
1 lb / 450 g scallops

MARINADE FOR PRAWNS AND SCALLOPS

juice of 1 lemon and 4 limes
3 cloves garlic, coarsely chopped
4 small dried hot chili peppers, coarsely chopped
1/2 teaspoon coarse salt
2 tablespoons olive oil

RICE

6 tablespoons olive oil
6 tablespoons butter
2 cups chopped onion
3 large cloves garlic, minced
2 cups / 450 g long grain rice
1 cup coarsely chopped fresh coriander - optional
1 cup coarsely chopped flat-leaved parsley - optional
3 - 4 cups / 0.7 - 1 litre chicken stock
1/2 tablespoons saffron
1 teaspoon salt

3 large red and/or yellow bell peppers
olive oil
12 fresh clams, unopened
12 fresh oysters, unopened
12 large fresh mussels, unopened
1 lb / 450 hot Polish, Cajun, or other spicy sausages
tabasco sauce

1 *Remove the heads and legs from the prawns, leaving the shells intact. Combine the marinade ingredients. Pour some over the prawns and marinate for 3 - 4 hours, and the rest over the scallops and marinate for 1 hour. When ready to grill, remove the prawns and scallops from the marinade and reserve the marinade.*

2 *Prepare the rice while waiting for the grill to reach the right temperature. Heat the oil and butter, sauté the garlic and onion for 5 minutes, then add the rice and salt and sauté until golden. Stir in the coriander and parsley, if using. Bring the stock to a boil, stir in the saffron and pour over the rice, just covering it. Cover the saucepan and boil for 1 minute. Lower the heat and simmer for 20 minutes. Remove from the heat and allow to stand, with the lid on, for 10 minutes. The rice should absorb all the liquid.*

3 *Brush the peppers with olive oil. Place on the grill over a medium heat and cook until the skins begin to blacken. When cool, remove the skins and cut the flesh into thin, even strips.*

4 *Prick the sausages, place them on the grill, and cook until they brown nicely and are done inside.*

5 *Brush the prawns and scallops with olive oil and place on the grill. Cook for about 2 minutes on each side. Peel the prawns and halve the sausages.*

6 *Place the clams, oysters, and mussels on the grill over a medium heat and cook until the shells begin to open.*

7 *Cut the sausages into thick slices. Mix with the rice, prawns, and scallops, adding the reserved marinade from the prawns and scallops and a dash of tabasco sauce. Decorate with the clams, oysters, and mussels still in their shells and garnish with the strips of pepper. Serve hot or at room temperature.*

❦ **SERVES 6**

SOFT-SHELLED CRABS WITH BROWNED BUTTER

- Browned Butter (see recipe below)
- 12 - 18 soft-shelled crabs, well cleaned
- 4 scallions (green or spring onions), thinly sliced
- 1 - 2 chili peppers, thinly sliced - optional
- salt and freshly ground pepper

1 *Prepare the Browned Butter, using just 1 cup / 225 g butter. Stir in the scallions and chili peppers (if using), and season with salt and pepper.*

2 *Place the crabs on an oiled grill over a medium heat and brush well with the Browned Butter. Cook for 3 - 4 minutes on each side, brushing occasionally with more Browned Butter, until crisp and a deep reddish brown. Serve the crabs with the remaining Browned Butter poured over them.*

❦ **SERVES 6**

BROWNED BUTTER

A SIMPLE SAUCE, EXCELLENT WITH FISH

- 2 cups / 450 g butter
- juice of 1 or 2 limes or lemons
- tabasco sauce
- salt and freshly ground pepper

1 *Melt the butter until it starts to froth and take on a dark brown color and nutty smell. Stir in lime or lemon juice to taste. Season with tabasco sauce, salt, and pepper, also to taste.*

2 *Keep hot in a small saucepan on the side of the grill.*

❦ **MAKES ABOUT 2 CUPS / 450 ml**

CRABS WITH BLACK BEAN SAUCE

6 large or 18 blue (small) crabs

BLACK BEAN SAUCE

4 tablespoons salted black beans, rinsed and chopped
3 tablespoons minced garlic
1 cup / 225 ml fish stock or chicken stock
6 - 8 tablespoons dry sherry
2 tablespoons sesame or vegetable oil
1/4 cup / 50 g butter
1 - 2 teaspoons tabasco sauce, to taste
chopped scallions (green or spring onions), to garnish

1 *Soak the crabs in salted water to remove the sand.*

2 *Place the crabs on the grill over a medium heat. Cook, turning once, until the shells turn pink (this means that the meat inside is cooked).*

3 *Heat the oil and butter in a small skillet (frying pan) on the grill. Add the black beans and garlic, and cook until the garlic becomes fragrant. Stir in the remaining sauce ingredients and cook until reduced to taste. Serve in individual bowls with a garnish of chopped scallion.*

Crab tongs and long thin forks are essential for dealing with undressed crabs. Browned Butter (see page 87) is also a good dipping sauce for crab; crab served in this way with Grilled Artichokes (see recipe page 129) makes a delicious starter.

❦ **SERVES 6**

GRILLED LOBSTERS

6 live lobsters (1 per person)
Browned Butter (see recipe page 77)

1 *Bring a large pot of water to a boil - use a pot large enough to hold several lobsters at once. Plunge the live lobsters into the water and bring to a boil again. Lower the heat, cover the pot, and cook for about 3 minutes or until the lobsters turn pink (not red). Immediately plunge the lobsters into cold water to stop them cooking.*

2 *Drain the lobsters well. Split them in half lengthwise, one large pincer to each half. With a small knife, remove the intestines, the vein running the length of the abdomen, and the sandy sac beneath the eyes.*

3 *Prepare the Browned Butter, using 1 lb / 450 g butter.*

4 *Place the lobster halves shell side down on the grill and brush liberally with Browned Butter. Cook over a medium heat, basting frequently with the Browned Butter until the shells turn bright red. Turn the lobsters over and cook for another 4 - 5 minutes. Turn again. When the meat is white, the lobsters are ready eat. Serve in their shells with the rest of the Browned Butter as a dipping sauce.*

❦ **SERVES 6**

GRILLED PRAWNS

MARINADE
3/4 cup / 175 ml melted butter
4 tablespoons olive oil
3 tablespoons chili sauce
2 tablespoons Worcestershire sauce
2 tablespoons grated zest of lemon
2 tablespoons fresh lemon juice
3 cloves garlic, minced
4 tablespoons minced parsley
1 teaspoon cayenne pepper
tabasco sauce, to taste
1 teaspoon herbes de Provence (fresh thyme, rosemary, bay, basil, and savory)
salt and freshly ground pepper
3 lbs / 1.4 kg large prawns, unpeeled
soaked bamboo skewers - optional

1 *Put all the marinade ingredients into a small saucepan and allow to simmer for 10 minutes. Season with salt and pepper to taste and allow to cool. Slit the prawns down the back. Pour the marinade over them and toss well. Marinate in the refrigerator for 3 - 4 hours, turning now and again.*

2 *Remove the prawns from the marinade and reserve the marinade. Thread the prawns onto skewers, if desired. Place on an oiled grill over a medium low heat until the shells turn pink. Pour the reserved marinade into a small saucepan on the side of the grill to heat up. Serve with the prawns as a dipping sauce.*

❦ **SERVES 6**

MIXED SHELLFISH ROAST

8 fresh oysters, 8 fresh clams, and 2 blue (small) crabs per person
2 cups / 450 g melted butter
salt and freshly ground pepper
lemons or limes, cut into wedges
tabasco sauce
green salad and crusty bread

1 *Soak the oysters, clams, and crabs in salted water for about 1 hour to remove the sand.*

2 *Place some of each on the grill over a medium heat. The crabs will cook in about 8 minutes and the clams and oysters will take 4 - 6 minutes for their shells to open. Keep cooking until everyone has satisfied their appetite!*

3 *Give everyone a small bowl of melted butter, and have salt, pepper, lemon wedges, and tabasco sauce ready on the buffet table. Serve with a green salad and crusty bread.*

This is messy food, so provide plenty of napkins!

GRILLED SCALLOPS

MARINADE

8 tablespoons dry white wine
3/4 teaspoon coarse salt
1 hot fresh chili pepper, seeded and minced
3 cloves garlic, minced
juice and grated zest of 2 lemons or limes
4 tablespoons olive oil

2 lbs / 450 g fresh scallops without shells
olive oil
soaked bamboo skewers
balsamic, sherry or red wine vinegar - optional
mixed fresh herbs, chopped

1 *Combine all the marinade ingredients and pour over the scallops. Marinate for 2 hours or overnight.*

2 *Remove the scallops from the marinade and reserve the marinade. Brush the scallops well with olive oil and thread onto skewers. Place on an oiled grill over a medium heat. Cook until lightly browned on all sides, but do not overcook. Mix a little olive oil (and vinegar, if desired) with the reserved marinade, and heat on the side of the grill to reduce it a little. Stir in the fresh herbs. Pour the sauce over the scallops, or serve in small bowls as a dipping sauce.*

❦ **SERVES 6**

STUFFED CALAMARI

24 calamari (baby squid), 4 - 6 inches / 10 - 15 cm long, cleaned, with tentacles

STUFFING

- 1 cup chopped parsley
- 3/4 cup / 175 g grated Parmesan cheese
- 1 egg, lightly beaten
- 1 - 2 tablespoons Zhoug Relish (see recipe page 23)
- olive oil
- salt and freshly ground pepper
- 3 cloves garlic or 3 shallots, chopped
- 10 peeled prawns or 8 oz / 225 g chopped Westphalian ham **OR** lachs schinken - optional
- 1 cup Lemon and Mustard Dressing (see recipe page 54)

1 *Coarsely chop the tentacles and mix them with the stuffing ingredients, adding enough olive oil to make a coarse paste. Add prawns or chopped ham, if desired. Stuff the bodies with this mixture.*

2 *Place the stuffed calamari on an oiled grill over a medium heat. Cook for about 2 minutes on each side, until the flesh turns white and opaque, and the stuffing is cooked.*

3 *Place the stuffed calamari in a shallow serving platter. Pour the Lemon and Mustard Dressing over them and serve hot. Alternatively, allow the calamari to marinate for several hours or overnight, turning them a few times, and serve cold the next day.*

A tasty alternative to Lemon and Mustard Dressing would be to blend together the juice of 2 or 3 lemons, 2 or 3 finely sliced shallots or cloves of garlic, a little balsamic or sherry vinegar, olive oil, salt, and pepper. If you decide to use Westphalian ham in the stuffing, save a little to strew on the top to serve.

❦ **SERVES 6**

Poultry

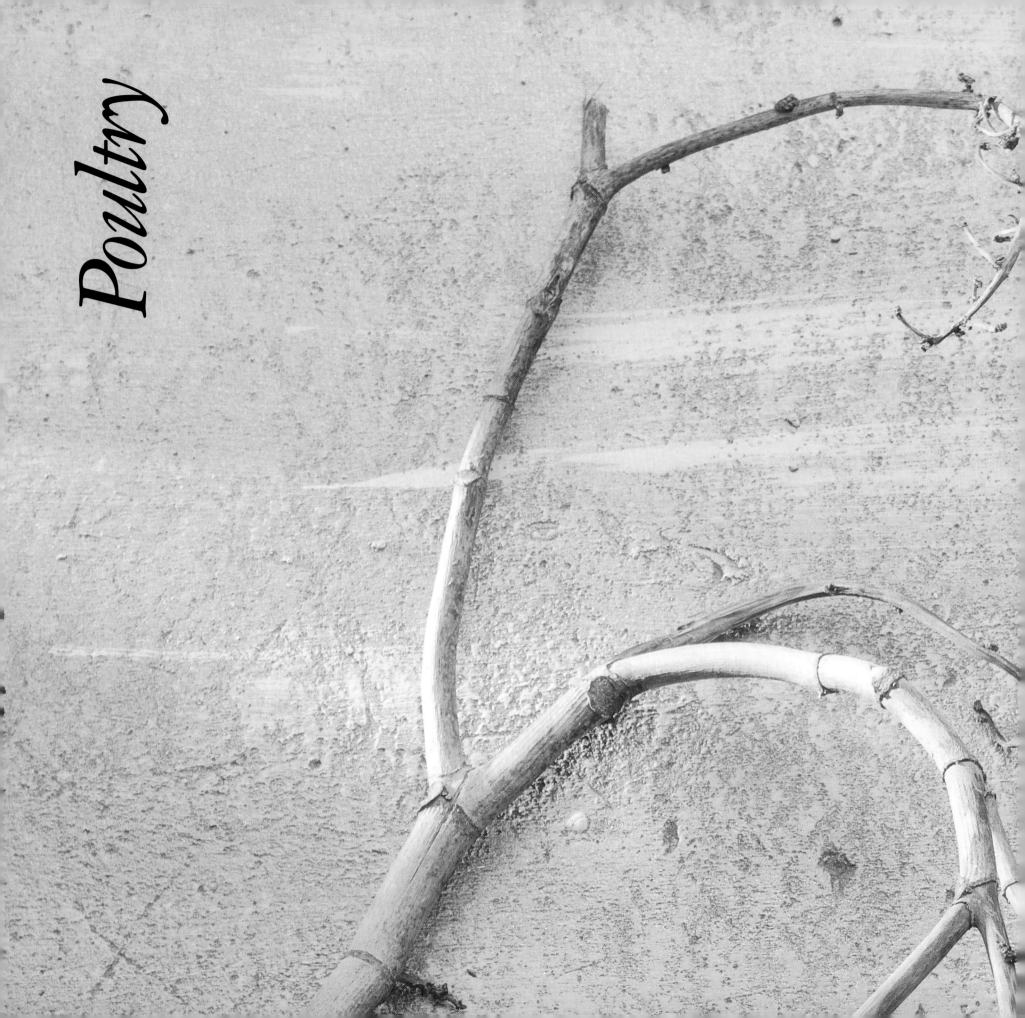

A CHICKEN THAT HAS NOT BEEN COOKED

WITH LOVE IS A CHICKEN THAT

HAS DIED IN VAIN.

Lin Yutang

Chinese-American essayist

(1895 - 1976)

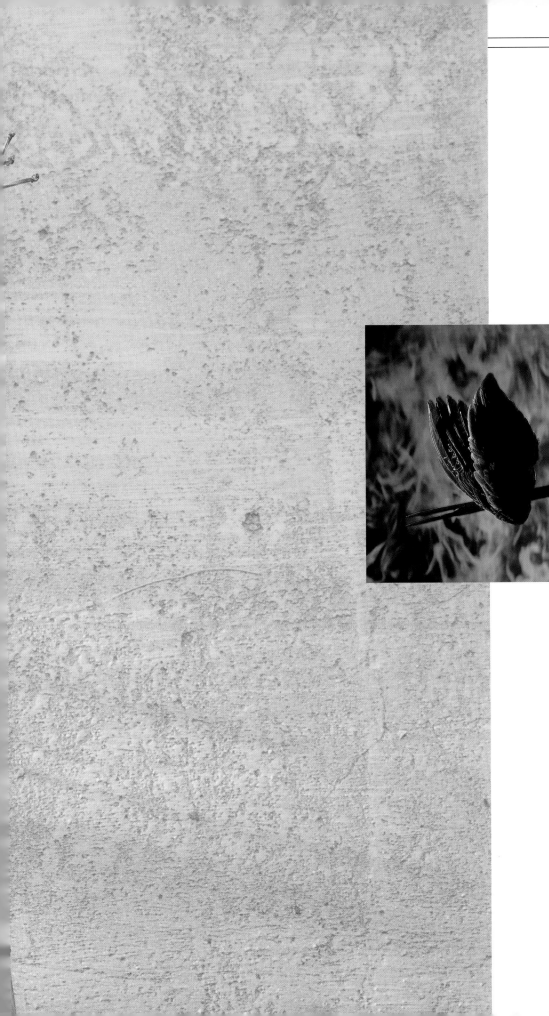

CHAPTER FIVE

Poultry

About 7,000 years ago, the people of Harappa, a city in the Indus Valley, were plagued by wild, stub-winged birds that were forever pecking at their crops. The discovery that the birds tasted good solved the problem. We are all in the debt of the Harappans for, once domesticated, these troublesome birds evolved into the ubiquitous chicken.

❦ *The truest challenge of a cook is to make chicken less boring than its reputation. This is not difficult if you are cooking on the grill. Not only does chicken have a natural affinity for smoke, it also manages to turn crisp on the outside and stay moist and juicy inside. Turkey is also ideal for grilling. By a very narrow margin, my favorite recipe in this book is the one for grilled turkey breast on page 97.*

❦ *A few hints for grilling poultry. Always allow the meat to come to room temperature before grilling, then grill it straight away (bacteria multiply rapidly in meat that is left to stand at room temperature). If you leave the skin on, be sure to rub marinade or spices under it. If your poultry portions are skinless, they will cook more rapidly, so be sure to watch them carefully and baste them frequently.*

RECIPES

Poultry

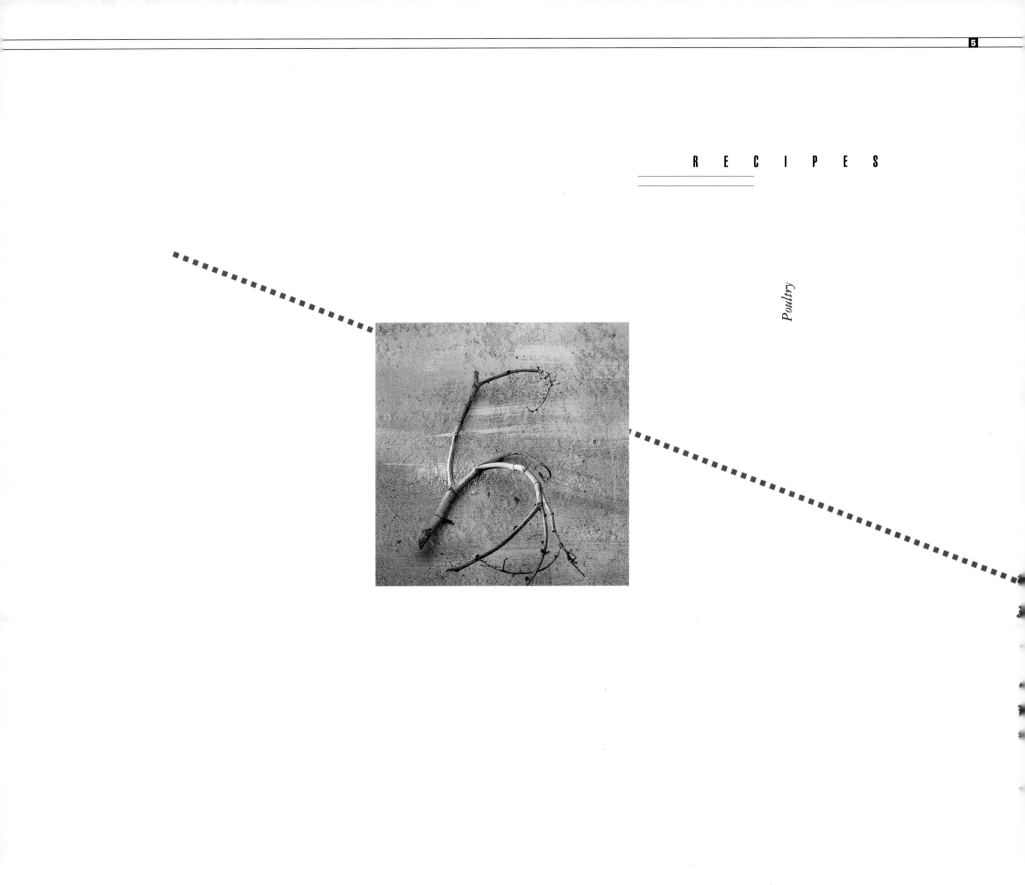

DUCK SOUTHEAST-ASIAN STYLE

MARINADE

- 8 cloves garlic
- 8 large scallions (green or spring onions), white part only
- 3 - 4 chili peppers, with or without seeds
- 4 teaspoons sugar
- 1 cup fresh coriander leaves
- 1 cup fresh basil leaves
- 1 teaspoon freshly ground pepper
- 4 tablespoons nuoc mam (Vietnamese fish sauce)
- 4 tablespoons soy sauce

DIPPING SAUCE

- 3 cloves garlic, crushed
- 1 - 2 chili peppers, seeded and minced
- 3 tablespoons fresh lime or lemon juice
- 6 tablespoons rice vinegar or wine vinegar
- 6 tablespoons nuoc mam

- 6 duck (or moullard) breasts weighing 6 - 8 oz / 175 - 225 g each, boned, skinned and pounded flat
- vegetable or sesame oil

1 *Place all the marinade ingredients in a food processor and blend to a rough paste. Rub the paste into the duck breasts. Marinate for several hours or overnight, turning several times.*

2 *Mix together the ingredients for the dipping sauce.*

3 *Remove the duck breasts from the marinade and brush them with vegetable or sesame oil. Place them on an oiled grill over a medium high heat and cook for 4 - 6 minutes on each side. Slice and serve with the dipping sauce.*

SERVES 6

DUCK OR CHICKEN LIVERS WITH HERBED BUTTER

2 lbs / 900 g duck or chicken livers, trimmed
2 tablespoons olive oil
salt and freshly ground pepper

HERBED BUTTER

3/4 cup / 175 g butter
3 cloves garlic, minced
4 shallots, minced
4 tablespoons chopped fresh sage or thyme
4 tablespoons chopped flat parsley
2 tablespoons Dijon mustard
4 tablespoons snipped chives
2 tablespoons fresh lemon or lime juice
salt and freshly ground pepper
pinch cayenne pepper

soaked bamboo skewers
fresh chives, to garnish

1 *Toss the livers with the olive oil and season with salt and pepper.*

2 *Melt the butter and stir in the rest of the Herbed Butter ingredients, seasoning to taste with salt, pepper, and cayenne.*

3 *Skewer the livers and place themon an oiled grill over a medium high heat. Cook for 2 minutes on each side, basting well with the Herbed Butter. Pour the remaining Herbed Butter over the livers to serve. Garnish with snipped chives.*

❦ **SERVES 6 TO 8**

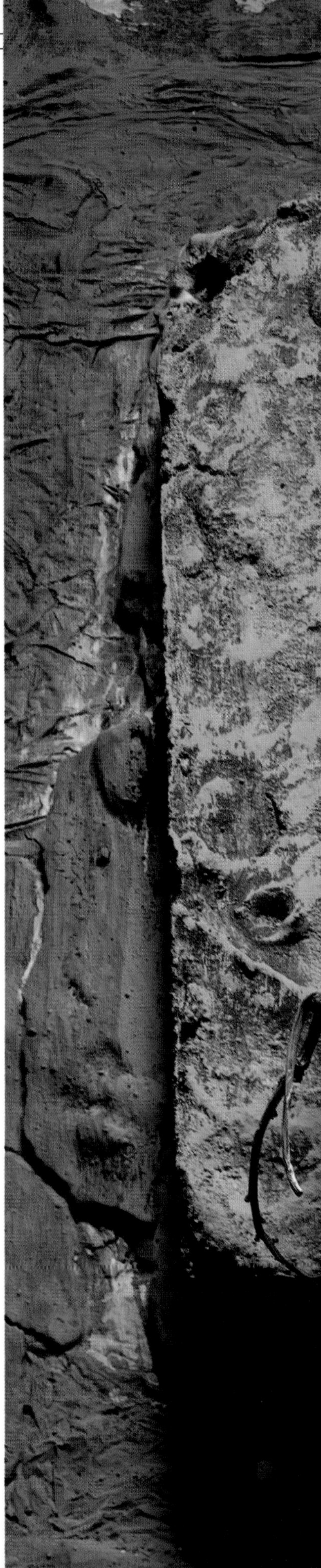

LEMON DUCK WITH CHILI SAUCE

MARINADE

- 8 scallions (green or spring onions), finely chopped
- 3 cloves garlic, minced
- 2 teaspoons minced fresh ginger
- 4 tablespoons soy sauce
- 2 teaspoons sugar
- 1 teaspoon salt
- 1 teaspoon freshly ground pepper
- 2 tablespoons grated zest of lemon

- 3 small ducks

CHILI SAUCE

- 1 cup / 225 ml nuoc mam (Vietnamese fish sauce)
- 1 tablespoon minced fresh ginger
- 4 cloves garlic, minced
- 2 - 3 hot fresh chili peppers, finely chopped
- 4 tablespoons lemon juice
- 2 tablespoons sugar
- 4 tablespoons water

1 *Mix together the Chili Sauce ingredients and refrigerate. Combine the marinade ingredients. Split the ducks in half and remove the backbone. Pour the marinade over the duck halves and refrigerate for at least 4 hours or overnight, turning occasionally.*

2 *Remove the duck halves from the marinade and reserve the marinade. Place the ducks skin side down on an oiled grill over a medium heat. Cook for about 40 minutes until evenly cooked and crisp, turning a few times and basting with the reserved marinade. Serve with individual bowls of Chili Sauce.*

❦ **SERVES 6**

CHICKEN WITH PEACHES

- 6 Cornish game hens, squabs, or spring chickens

MARINADE

- 1 cup / 225 ml fresh lemon juice
- 4 tablespoons honey
- 2 - 4 dried red chili peppers (with or without seeds), chopped
- 1 teaspoon salt
- 1/2 teaspoon freshly ground pepper

- 1 cup / 225 g butter
- 6 peaches, peeled, halved and pitted

1 *Split the birds and remove the backbone. Mix together the marinade ingredients and pour over the birds. Marinate for at least 4 hours or overnight, turning occasionally.*

2 *Heat the butter over a medium low heat until it begins to foam, then turn brown, with a nutty smell. Remove the birds from the marinade and reserve the marinade. Stir the browned butter into it and heat on the side of the grill.*

3 *Place the birds on an oiled grill over a medium heat. Baste frequently with the butter sauce until done (6 - 8 minutes per side, depending on the size of the birds). Meanwhile, dip the peach halves in the butter mixture, place them on the grill, and cook for 10 minutes, basting frequently. Arrange the birds and peaches on a serving platter and pour the sauce over them.*

❦ **SERVES 6**

CHICKEN BREASTS WITH LEMON AND MUSTARD

LEMON MUSTARD MARINADE
4 tablespoons Dijon mustard
1/2 cup / 100 ml fresh lemon juice
2 tablespoons zest of lemon, finely chopped
1 teaspoon salt
1/2 teaspoon freshly ground pepper
1/4 - 1/2 teaspoon cayenne pepper
1 cup chopped fresh coriander
1 cup chopped parsley
4 chicken breasts, boned and halved

1 *Mix together all the marinade ingredients. Pour over the halved chicken breasts and marinate for at least 4 hours.*

2 *Remove the chicken from the marinade and reserve the marinade. Place on an oiled grill over a medium heat and grill for about 3 minutes on each side, basting occasionally with the marinade.*

Many other fresh herbs, or mixtures of herbs, can be used instead of coriander and parsley.

❦ **SERVES 6**

CORNISH GAME HENS WITH CITRUS, SOY, AND CREAM SAUCE

MARINADE
1 large onion, thinly sliced
1 cup / 225 ml soy sauce
8 scallions (green or spring onions), thinly sliced
1/2 cup / 100 ml orange juice
1/2 cup / 100 ml red wine vinegar
1/2 cup / 100 ml chicken stock
1/2 cup / 100 ml lemon juice
2 tablespoons fresh ginger, minced
1 cup coarsely chopped fresh coriander
6 Cornish game hens, squabs, or spring chickens,
split and with backbone removed
1 cup / 225 ml cream

1 *Mix together all the marinade ingredients and pour over the birds. Marinate in the refrigerator overnight, turning several times.*

2 *Remove the birds from the marinade and reserve 1/2 cup / 100 ml of the marinade for basting. Bring the rest of the marinade to a boil, then simmer until reduced to half. Stir in the cream and keep warm.*

3 *Place the birds on an oiled grill over a medium heat. Cook for about 8 minutes on each side, basting with the reserved marinade. Pour the cream sauce over the birds to serve.*

❦ **SERVES 6**

SPICY CHICKEN

SPICE RUB

- 1 - 2 teaspoons salt
- 1 teaspoon freshly ground black pepper
- 1 teaspoon freshly ground white pepper
- 1 teaspoon cayenne pepper
- 1 teaspoon dried mustard
- 6 tablespoons fresh or 6 teaspoons dried thyme or oregano
- 2 - 4 bayleaves, crumbled
- 5 cloves garlic, minced

- 5 lbs / 2.25 kg chicken (breasts, wings, thighs, drumsticks)
- olive oil

1 *Combine all the spices and herbs, and rub well into the chicken pieces, especially under the skin. Set aside for at least 2 hours' or overnight.*

2 *Place the chicken on an oiled grill over a medium heat. Cook until well browned and crispy (8 - 15 minutes on each side, depending on the size of the pieces), basting with olive oil and turning occasionally.*

❦ **SERVES 8**

CHICKEN WITH BRANDY

MARINADE

- 3 lemons, thinly sliced
- 6 shallots, sliced
- 1 cup / 225 ml olive oil
- 2/3 cup / 150 ml brandy
- 12 sprigs fresh thyme or oregano
- salt and freshly ground pepper
- pinch cayenne pepper

- 5 lbs / 2.25 kg chicken (breasts, thighs, or drumsticks)
- 1 cup ripe (black) oil-cured olives
- 1 cup green olives

1 *Mix together the marinade ingredients, pour over the chicken, and toss well. Marinate in the refrigerator overnight, turning several times.*

2 *Remove the chicken from the marinade, reserving the marinade. Place the chicken on an oiled grill over a medium heat. Cooking time depends on the size of the portions, but 6 - 8 minutes per side should be enough.*

3 *Heat the reserved marinade on the side of the grill to reduce it a little. Arrange the chicken pieces on a serving platter and pour the reduced marinade over them.*

❦ **SERVES 8**

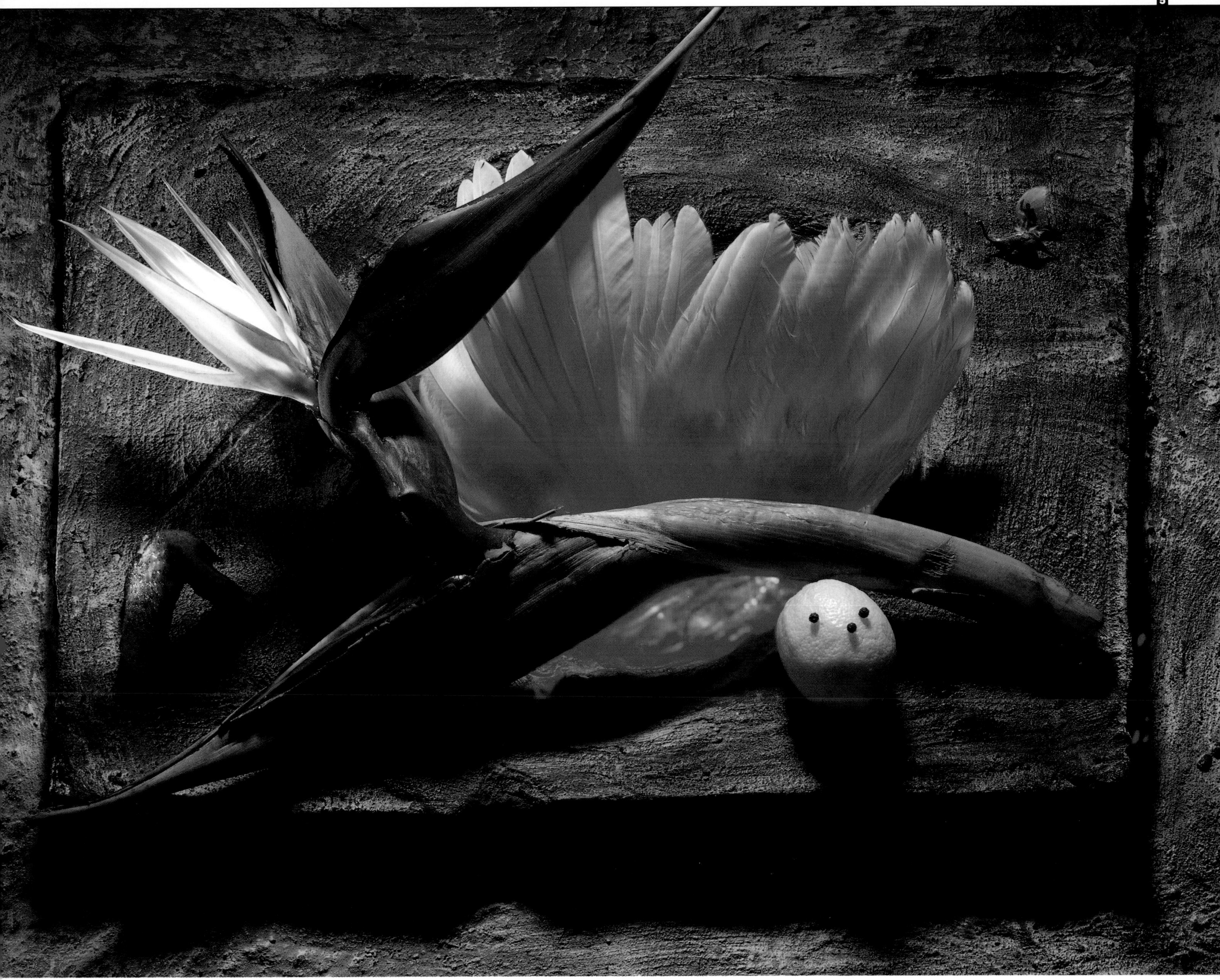

GRILLED TURKEY BREAST

MARINADE
1 cup / 225 ml dry white wine
1 cup / 225 ml cider or wine vinegar
2 cups / 450 ml brandy
2 tablespoons sugar
2 teaspoons freshly ground pepper
1 1/2 tablespoons mustard seed
1 tablespoon pickling spice - optional
3 tablespoons fresh rosemary, crushed
3 tablespoons fresh sage or thyme
3 tablespoons chopped garlic
1/2 cup / 100 ml oil
1 1/2 teaspoons coarse salt
1 - 2 turkey breasts, skinned and boned
salt and freshly ground pepper
olive oil

1 *Mix together the wine, vinegar, brandy, sugar, pepper, mustard seed, and pickling spice, and bring to a boil over a high heat. Simmer until the liquid is reduced to half. Allow to cool to room temperature.*

2 *Add the herbs and other marinade ingredients. Pour over the turkey breasts and turn to coat well. Marinate in the refrigerator for at least two days (or up to seven), turning occasionally.*

3 *Remove the turkey breasts from the marinade and reserve the marinade. Season the meat with salt and pepper, and brush with oil.*

4 *Place the turkey breasts on an oiled grill over a low heat. Cook for about 25 minutes, turning frequently and basting with the reserved marinade. Place the reserved marinade in a small pan and reduce it to half. Slice the turkey breasts thinly and serve with the reduced marinade. Delicious served warm or at room temperature.*

Leftovers of grilled turkey breast are marvelous in salads and sandwiches.

❦ **SERVES 6**

GOOSE LIVER WITH WARM VINAIGRETTE

VINAIGRETTE

6 tablespoons red wine or balsamic vinegar
4 shallots, finely chopped
3 tablespoons chopped flat parsley
salt and freshly ground pepper
6 tablespoons walnut or olive oil

2 lbs / 900 g goose liver, cut into slices
1 inch / 2.5 cm thick
olive oil
salt and freshly ground pepper
snipped chives, to garnish

1 *Pour the vinegar into a small saucepan and add the shallots, herbs, salt, and pepper. Cook over a medium heat, or on the side of the grill, for 1 minute, then stir in the 6 tablespoons of walnut or olive oil. Remove from the heat but keep warm.*

2 *Brush the slices of goose liver with oil and season with salt and pepper. Place on an oiled grill over a medium heat. Cook for about 40 seconds on each side. Serve with the warm vinaigrette and a sprinkling of chives.*

❦ **SERVES 6 TO 8**

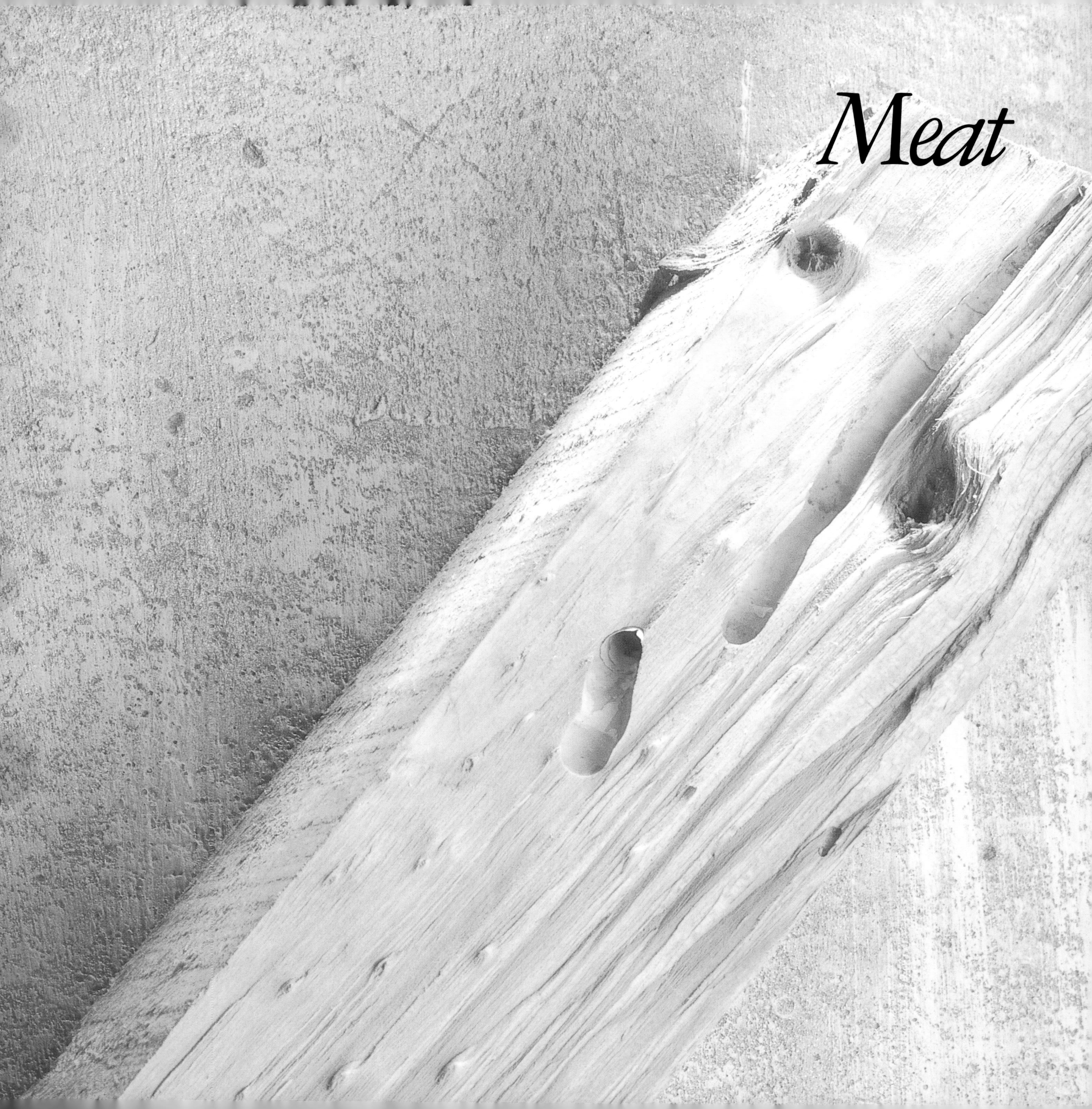

Meat

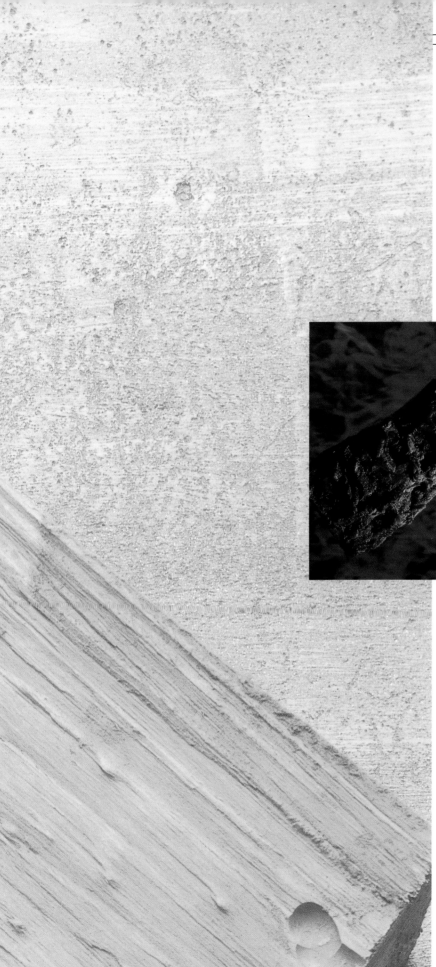

MENTION MEAT TO DEDICATED CARNIVORES AND THE FIRST THING THEY THINK OF IS STEAK. STEAK IS THE SOUL OF MEAT, THE TRUEST AND THE MOST INDISPENSABLE PART OF MEAT.

Roland Barthes

French literary critic

(1915 - 1980)

CHAPTER SIX

Meat

Mention meat to gourmets and, in addition to images of steak, they see in their mind's eye racks of lamb, veal cutlets, and pork chops. Despite a host of medical curmudgeons, meat is important to human beings. Meat, in a phrase, is delicious. And meat is often at its best when grilled.

❦ *Only the most tender cuts of meat should be used for grilling and they should be allowed to come to room temperature before being grilled. Grill your meat as quickly as possible thereafter.*

❦ *Although many cookbooks suggest turning meat on the grill only once, I believe in turning and basting more frequently. This helps to keep all the natural juices in. Nearly all meats should be quickly seared on all sides over hot coals and then moved to a cooler part of the grill to continue cooking.*

❦ *Steaks should be 1 1/2 - 2 inches (4 - 5 cm) thick and of prime or top quality, with a fine marbling of fat. Large steaks and other large pieces of meat should be carved before serving, and always allowed to "rest" for about 10 minutes before carving.*

RECIPES

Meat

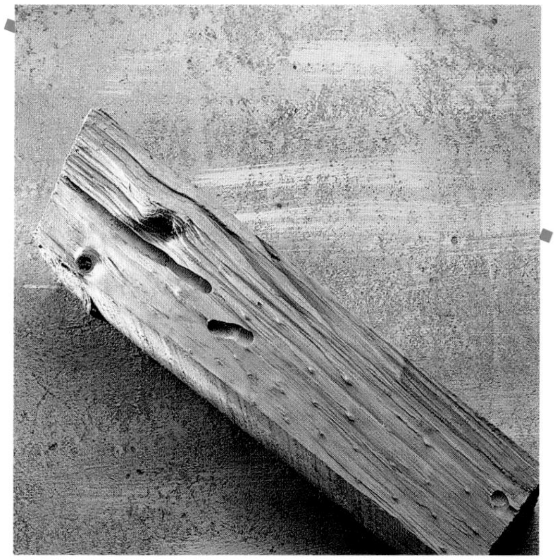

FILLET OF BEEF WITH MUSTARD CRUST

- a whole fillet of beef (about 4 lbs / 1.8 kg)
- 4 - 6 cloves garlic, cut into slivers
- salt and freshly ground pepper
- 8 - 10 tablespoons Dijon mustard
- 4 tablespoons olive oil

1 *Make plenty of slits in the meat and insert the slivers of garlic. Season well with salt and pepper. Coat the meat in the mustard and set aside for at least 4 hours or overnight.*

2 *Just before grilling, brush the fillet with olive oil. Place on a well - oiled grill over a medium high heat. Cook for about 15 minutes if you like your beef rare, longer if you prefer it well done. Turn the meat occasionally and baste with olive oil.*

3 *Transfer the meat to a cutting board. Let it rest for 10 minutes before carving into slices.*

To prevent the tail of the fillet from overcooking and drying out, tuck it under and secure it with a toothpick.
Beef fillet is also excellent with mushrooms (a mixture of wild, shitake, oyster, etc.). Skewer the mushrooms, brush them with olive oil, dust with salt and pepper, and grill until browned and tender.

❦ **SERVES 6 TO 8**

LEMON PEPPER STEAK

- 3 lbs / 1.3 kg sirloin or New York steak
- 2 tablespoons freshly ground pepper
- 4 tablespoons dried chili pepper flakes
- 4 tablespoons fresh oregano or 4 teaspoons dried
- 1 cup / 225 ml fresh lemon juice
- 3/4 cup / 175 ml olive oil
- salt

1 *Cut the meat into steaks or leave in one piece. Spread the pepper on a plate and press the meat into it on both sides.*

2 *Combine the remaining ingredients and pour over the meat. Marinate for at least 4 hours, turning occasionally.*

3 *Remove the meat from the marinade and reserve the marinade. Season the meat with salt, then place it on an oiled grill over a medium heat. Sear the meat on both sides, then move it to a slightly cooler part of the grill (or raise the grill rack). Steaks 1 1/2 - 2 inches / 4 - 5 cm thick will take another 4 - 6 minutes to cook; if you are cooking your steak whole, allow about 15 minutes.*

❦ **SERVES 6**

BEEF WITH HERB AND PEPPER CRUST

HERB AND PEPPER CRUST

- 5 tablespoons lemon juice
- 2 tablespoons grated zest of lemon
- 3 tablespoons olive oil
- 4 tablespoons minced fresh rosemary
- 4 tablespoons minced fresh thyme
- 2 tablespoons black peppercorns
- 1 teaspoon salt

- roasting joint of beef or steak, weighing 4 lbs / 1.8 kg
- olive oil

1 *Put all the crust ingredients into a food processor and blend to a coarse paste. Rub the paste into the meat and refrigerate overnight.*

2 *Remove the meat from the refrigerator 1 hour before grilling. Place on an oiled grilled over a medium heat and sear well on all sides. Raise the grill (or move the meat to a cooler part of the grill, or simply turn down the heat) and cook for a further 15 - 20 minutes (35 minutes for well done), turning occasionally and basting with olive oil. Allow the meat to rest for 10 minutes before carving.*

❦ **SERVES 8 TO 10**

STEAKS WITH MUSTARD AND HERB CRUST

MARINADE

- 1/2 cup / 100 ml lemon juice or balsamic, sherry, or red wine vinegar
- 3/4 cup / 175 ml olive oil
- 4 cloves garlic, minced

- 6 sirloin or New York steaks weighing about 8 oz / 225 g each
- 4 tablespoons Dijon mustard

HERB CRUST

- 1 tablespoon sweet Hungarian paprika
- 1 tablespoon crushed black peppercorns
- 1 1/2 teaspoons coarse salt
- 1 tablespoon minced fresh oregano
- 1 tablespoon minced fresh thyme
- 2 tablespoons minced flat-leaved parsley
- 1 teaspoon cayenne pepper
- 1 teaspoon fennel seeds

1 *Combine the marinade ingredients and pour over the steaks. Marinate for 4 hours or overnight, turning occasionally.Remove the steaks from the marinade, reserving the marinade. Spread the steaks with the mustard. Combine the ingredients for the herb crust rub and sprinkle over the steaks. Set aside for 1 hour.*

3 *Place the steaks on an oiled grill. Cook over a high heat for 4 - 6 minutes on each side.*

4 *Reduce the reserved marinade on the side of the grill to thicken, and pour over the meat to serve.*

❦ **SERVES 6**

HAMBURGERS WITH ROQUEFORT CHEESE

2 1/2 lbs / 1.25 kg ground (minced) beef
3 tablespoons Worcestershire sauce
3 tablespoons Dijon mustard
1 medium onion, chopped
salt and freshly ground pepper
8 oz / 225 g Roquefort cheese, crumbled
1/4 cup / 50 g butter, softened
fresh chives, snipped

1 *Mix together the ground beef, Worcestershire sauce, mustard, onion, salt, and pepper. Set aside. Mix together the cheese and butter.*

2 *Divide the hamburger mixture into 12 patties. Place a spoonful of cheese and butter on six of them and use the other six as "lids." With your fingertips, pinch the edges together to seal in the filling.*

3 *Place the filled hamburgers on an oiled grill over a medium heat. Cook for about 4 minutes on each side for rare, or 6 - 7 minutes for well done. Serve with a sprinkling of snipped chives.*

❦ **SERVES 6**

MIDDLE-EASTERN LAMB KEBABS

- 2 1/2 lbs / 1.2 kg ground (minced) lamb, with a little extra ground lamb fat
- 1 medium onion, finely chopped
- 2 - 4 cloves garlic, minced
- 1 cup finely chopped parsley
- 1 cup finely chopped fresh coriander
- 1 - 2 teaspoons salt
- 1 teaspoon each of freshly ground pepper, allspice, paprika, and cayenne pepper
- soaked bamboo skewers

1 *Mix together all the ingredients, adding more or less of the herbs and spices to taste.*

2 *Shape the mixture into sausages 3 inches / 8 cm long, molding each sausage around a skewer. Place the skewers on an oiled grill over a medium high heat and cook for 6 - 8 minutes, turning frequently. Serve in warm pita bread.*

❦ **MAKES ABOUT 18 SKEWERS**

LOIN LAMB CHOPS

MARINADE

- 1 teaspoon salt
- 4 cloves garlic, minced
- 1 - 2 tablespoons Worcestershire sauce
- 1 tablespoon wine vinegar
- 3 tablespoons olive oil
- freshly ground pepper

- 8 loin lamb chops

1 *Mix together the marinade ingredients and rub into the lamb chops. Marinate for at least 2 hours.*

2 *Remove the chops from the marinade and reserve the marinade. Place the chops on an oiled grill set about 4 inches / 10 cm above a medium heat. Grill for 4 - 6 minutes on each side, basting occasionally with the reserved marinade.*

❦ **SERVES 4**

MIXED SAUSAGE GRILL

- 4 - 5 lbs / 1.8 - 2.25 kg sausages (Italian, Polish, Cajun, etc, mixing mild and spicy)
- assorted mustards (grain, fine, herbed, etc.)

1 *Prick the skins of the sausages with the tip of a small, sharp knife.Brush the grill with oil and place the sausages on it. Cook, turning often, until the sausages are browned on all sides but still juicy inside. Serve with the various mustards.*

❦ **SERVES 8 TO 10**

LAMB TENDERLOIN WITH MINT BASTE

BASTE

4 - 6 cloves garlic
2 - 3 fresh chili peppers, seeded or unseeded
1 1/2 cups fresh mint
2 tablespoons Dijon or grain mustard
6 tablespoons wine vinegar
4 tablespoons olive oil

lamb tenderloin (fillet) weighing about 3 1/2 lbs / 1.6 kg, or two smaller tenderloins
salt and freshly ground pepper

1 *Put the garlic, chili peppers, and mint into a blender or food processor and mix to a coarse paste. Add the mustard, vinegar, and oil. Pour over the lamb, turning so it is coated on all sides. Marinate overnight in the refrigerator, turning occasionally.*

2 *Remove the lamb from the marinade and reserve the marinade. Season the lamb with salt and pepper. Place on an oiled grill over a medium high heat. Sear the meat on all sides for about 2 minutes, then turn down the heat (or move the meat to a cooler part of the grill or raise the grill rack). Cook for another 10 minutes (5 minutes if you are cooking two small tenderloins), turning occasionally and basting with the reserved marinade. Allow to rest for 5 minutes before carving.*

❦ **SERVES 6**

GRILLED LAMB'S LIVER

MARINADE

6 tablespoons olive oil
1 - 2 teaspoons cumin
2 teaspoons paprika
1/2 teaspoon cayenne pepper
1/2 teaspoon salt

2 1/2 lbs / 1.2 kg lamb's liver
soaked bamboo skewers
wine vinegar - optional
snipped chives, to garnish

1 *Mix together the ingredients for the marinade. Cut the liver into large cubes, pour the marinade over them, and marinate for at least 2 hours.*

2 *Remove the liver from the marinade, reserving the marinade. Thread the liver onto skewers and place on an oiled grill over a very high heat. Grill very quickly so that the outside of the liver is charred but the inside is pink, basting with the reserved marinade. Serve sprinkled with wine vinegar, if liked, and snipped chives.*

❦ **SERVES 6**

BUTTERFLIED LEG OF LAMB

MARINADE

3 large cloves garlic, minced
1 - 2 tablespoons dried or 15 sprigs fresh oregano
1 teaspoon coarsely ground black pepper
1 teaspoon coarse salt
2 tablespoons fresh lemon juice
4 tablespoons olive oil

leg of lamb (or 2 smaller legs) weighing
5 - 6 lbs / 2.2 - 2.7 kg, boned and butterflied
(see note)
6 tablespoons Dijon mustard - optional
olive oil

1 *Mix together all the marinade ingredients. Make 1/2-inch / 1-cm deep slits all over the lamb. Rub in the marinade, working it into the slits. Refrigerate overnight.*

3 *Remove the lamb from the refrigerator and drain. Spread the lamb with the mustard, if using, and allow the mustard to dry a little (about 45 minutes). Brush the lamb with olive oil and place on an oiled grill over a medium heat. Cook for 20 - 30 minutes for rare and 40 minutes for well done, turning occasionally and brushing with olive oil. Allow to rest for 10 minutes before carving.*

To "butterfly" a leg of lamb, cut it lengthwise through to the bone, remove the bone, and cut nearly through to the other side. The leg makes a butterfly shape when the two halves are opened out.

❦ **SERVES 8 TO 10**

LEG OF LAMB WITH MINT HONEY SAUCE

leg of lamb (or 2 smaller legs) weighing
4 - 5 lbs / 1.8 - 2.25 kg
2 cups / 600 ml Mint Honey Sauce
(see recipe page 54)

1 *Trim any excess fat off the lamb. Pour the marinade over the lamb and turn it several times to coat it thoroughly. Marinate in the refrigerator overnight, turning occasionally.*

2 *Remove the lamb from the marinade. Reserve the marinade. Place the lamb on an oiled grill set about 8 inches / 20 cm above a medium heat. Cook for about 40 minutes (less for smaller legs), turning occasionally and basting well with the reserved marinade. Allow the lamb to rest for 10 minutes before carving.*

Mint Honey Sauce can be prepared several days in advance.

❦ **SERVES 8 TO 10**

VEAL CHOPS WITH SAGE

MARINADE

1/2 cup / 100 ml olive oil

2 tablespoons wine vinegar or fresh lemon juice

2 - 4 cloves garlic, minced

2 tablespoons crushed fresh sage

salt and freshly ground pepper

6 veal chops, 1 1/2 inches / 3.5 cm thick

1 *Mix together all the marinade ingredients and rub well into the chops. Marinate for at least 4 hours, turning occasionally.*

2 *Remove the veal chops from the marinade. Reserve the marinade. Liberally season the chops with salt and pepper, and place them on an oiled grill over a medium high heat. Cook for about 4 minutes on each side, basting well with the reserved marinade.*

❦ **SERVES 6**

RACK OF LAMB WITH OREGANO

MARINADE

2 cups / 450 ml dry red wine

2/3 cup / 150 ml balsamic, sherry, or wine vinegar

1 cup / 225 ml olive oil

6 cloves garlic, minced

2 cups chopped fresh oregano

salt and freshly ground pepper

2 racks of lamb (containing 8 ribs each), cracked

1 *Combine the marinade ingredients and pour over the lamb. Refrigerate for 6 hours or overnight, turning several times.*

2 *Remove the lamb from the marinade, reserving the marinade. Place on an oiled grill over a medium heat and cook for about 10 minutes (15 minutes for well done), turning and basting occasionally with the reserved marinade. Pour the remaining marinade into a small saucepan on the side of the grill and reduce to a syrupy consistency, straining if desired. Separate the ribs and pour the marinade over them to serve.*

❦ **SERVES 6 TO 8**

VEAL CHOPS WITH HERBED BUTTER

HERBED BUTTER
3/4 cup / 150 g melted butter
3 tablespoons Dijon mustard
3 scallions (green or spring onions), finely chopped
6 tablespoons chopped fresh thyme or flat parsley
3 cloves garlic, finely minced
salt and freshly ground pepper
6 veal chops, 1 1/2 - 2 inches / 3.5 - 5 cm thick
olive or vegetable oil

1 *Mix together all the herbed butter ingredients, adding a generous amount of pepper. Put on the side of the grill to keep warm.*

2 *Brush the chops with oil and place on an oiled grill over a medium heat. Cook for 3 - 4 minutes on each side, basting liberally with the herbed butter. Serve with the remainder of the herbed butter.*

❦ **SERVES 6**

PORK TENDERLOIN WITH CHILI CURE

CHILI CURE
2 fresh chili peppers, chopped
1 onion, coarsely chopped
4 - 6 large cloves garlic
2 tablespoons chili powder
1 tablespoon coarse salt
1 tablespoon freshly ground pepper
2 tablespoons fresh or 2 teaspoons dried oregano
1 teaspoon cumin
2 tablespoons sugar
1 tablespoon wine vinegar
2 or 3 pork tenderloins (fillets), weighing about 3 lbs / 1.3 kg in total
olive oil

1 *Put the chili peppers, onion, and garlic in a blender or food processor and mix to a purée. Stir in the other cure ingredients. Rub the mixture well into the tenderloins and refrigerate overnight.*

2 *Take the meat out of the refrigerator 1 hour before grilling. Rub with olive oil and place on an oiled grill over a medium high heat. Quickly sear the meat on all sides, then move it to a cooler part of the grill (or turn the heat down or raise the grill rack) and continue cooking for 10 - 15 minutes, turning frequently and basting with olive oil. Allow the meat to rest for 5 minutes before carving.*

❦ **SERVES 6**

PORK TENDERLOIN SOUTHEAST-ASIAN STYLE

MARINADE

- 6 cloves garlic
- 8 scallions (green or spring onions), white part only
- 3 fresh chili peppers, seeded or unseeded
- 3 teaspoons sugar
- 1 cup fresh coriander
- 1 cup fresh basil
- 1 teaspoon freshly ground pepper
- 3 - 4 tablespoons nuoc mam (Vietnamese fish sauce)
- 3 - 4 tablespoons soy sauce

- 2 - 3 pork tenderloins (fillets), weighing about 3 lbs / 1.3 kg in total
- sesame or vegetable oil

DIPPING SAUCE

- 3 cloves garlic, crushed
- 1 - 2 fresh chili peppers, seeded and minced
- 2 tablespoons sugar
- 3 tablespoons fresh lime or lemon juice
- 6 tablespoons rice vinegar
- 6 tablespoons nuoc mam

1 *Mix the marinade ingredients to a coarse paste. Make several slits in the meat and rub the marinade into the slits and the meat. Marinate overnight in the refrigerator, turning occasionally.*

2 *Remove the pork from the marinade and reserve the marinade. Brush the meat with oil and place on an oiled grill over a medium high heat. Quickly sear the meat on all sides to seal it, then move it to a cooler part of the grill (or turn down the heat or raise the grill rack). Continue cooking the meat for 10 - 15 minutes, turning occasionally and basting with the reserved marinade. Allow the meat to stand for 5 minutes before carving.*

3 *While the meat is cooking, put the dipping sauce ingredients in a blender or food processor and mix to a smooth consistency. Set on the side of the grill to warm through. Serve with the sliced meat.*

❦ **SERVES 6**

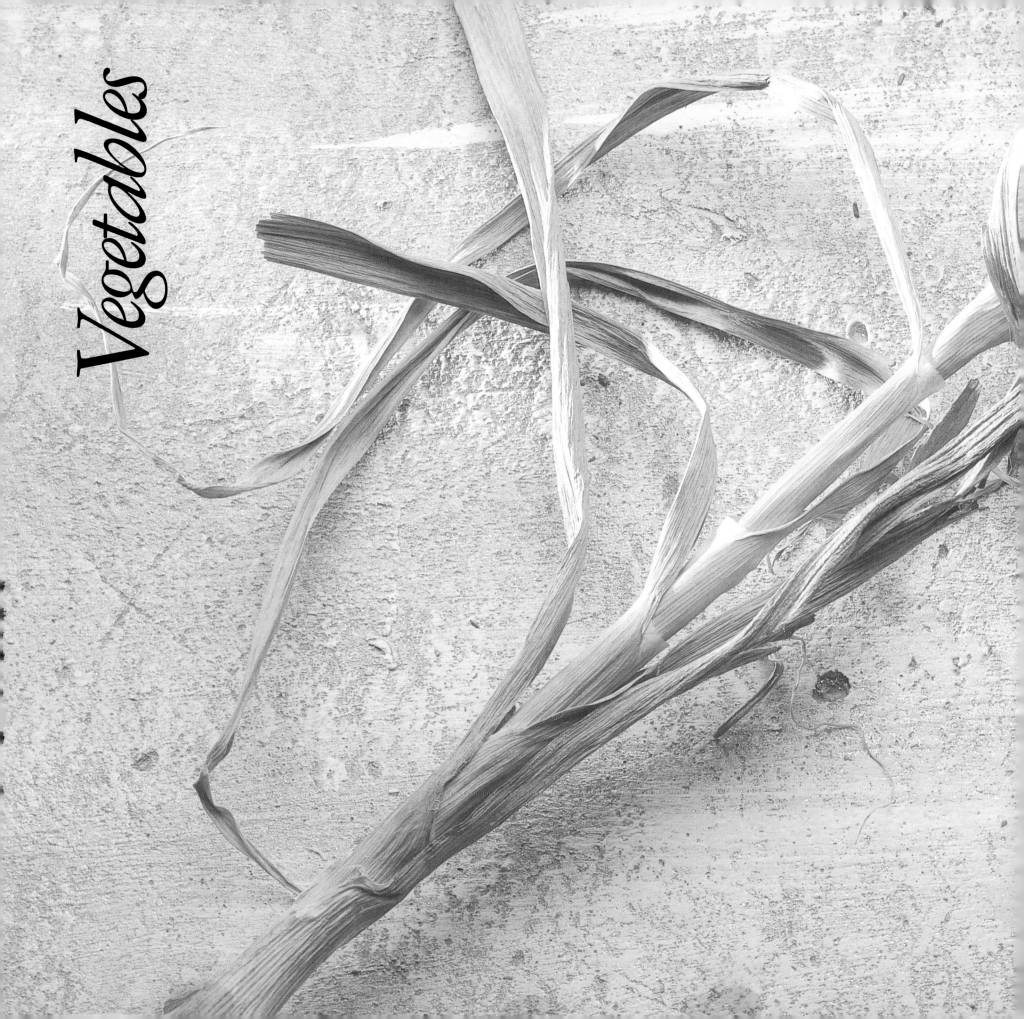

Vegetables

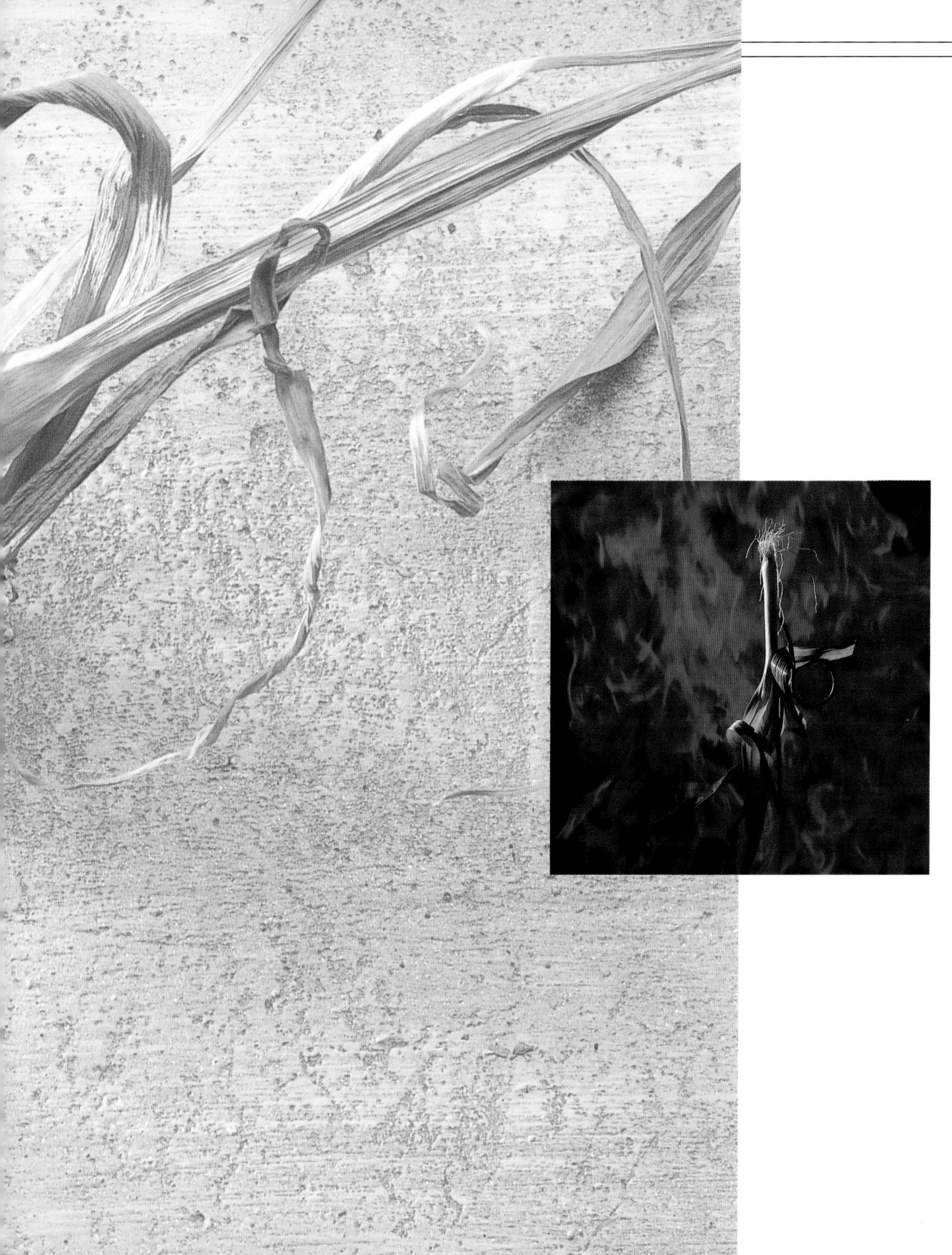

EARLY IN THE YEAR [THE STALLS OF VENICE] ARE BRIGHT WITH GREAT PILES OF PLUMP WHITE CAULIFLOWERS, AND RICH RED AND YELLOW LETTUCES. LATER, THE GREENY-PURPLE ARTICHOKES AND BLANCHED FENNEL ROOTS OF WINTER GRADUALLY GIVE WAY TO ENORMOUS WHITE STICKS OF SPRING ASPARAGUS AND SMOOTH DEEP PURPLE AUBERGINES. HIGH SUMMER BRINGS PILES OF GREEN ZUCCHINI WITH THEIR YELLOW FLOWERS, FLAME-RED TOMATOES, THE MYRIAD VARIETIES OF MUSHROOMS....

Lawrence Durrell

English novelist,

(1912 - 1990)

CHAPTER SEVEN

Vegetables

Almost all vegetables are ideally suited to the grill. Whether served on their own or as side dishes with grilled fish, poultry, or meat, the variety offered by the vegetable kingdom is nearly endless.

❦ *Whether you like your vegetables sliced or whole, select only perfect, unblemished specimens, and leave the skins on (the skins add color and also contain vitamins). Marinated slowly and lovingly, or simply brushed with oil and put straight on the grill, vegetables should be turned and basted while being grilled. When cooked they should be crisply tender and nicely browned.*

❦ *With good olive oil, wedges of lemon, and fresh herbs, a plate of firm, fresh vegetables can look and taste marvelous. Combine your vegetables so that their colors contrast, but don't use too many different flavors. When making up a platter, imagine how the finished arrangement will look.*

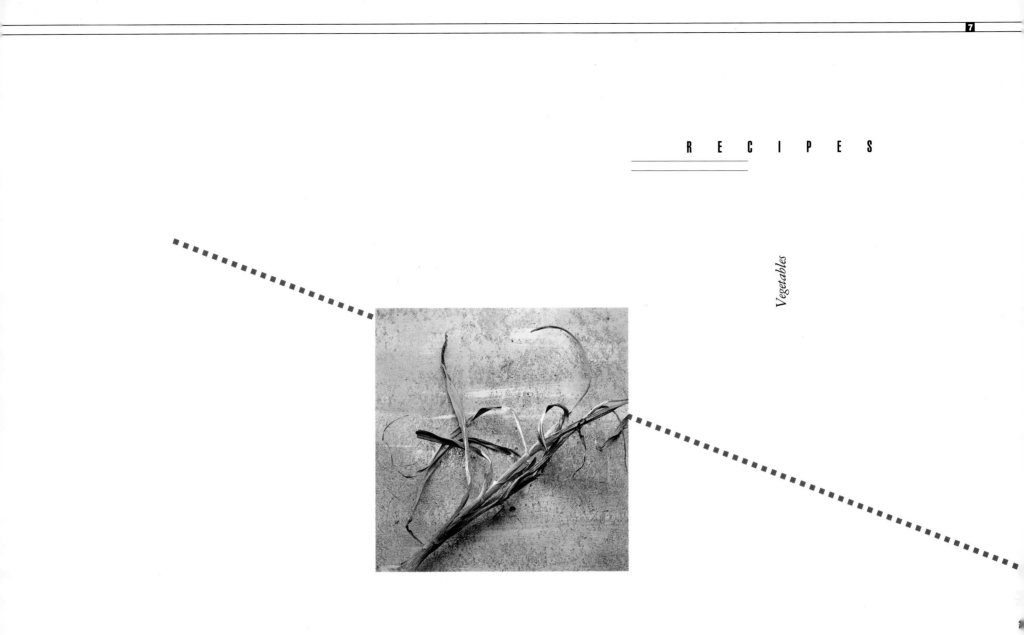

RECIPES

Vegetables

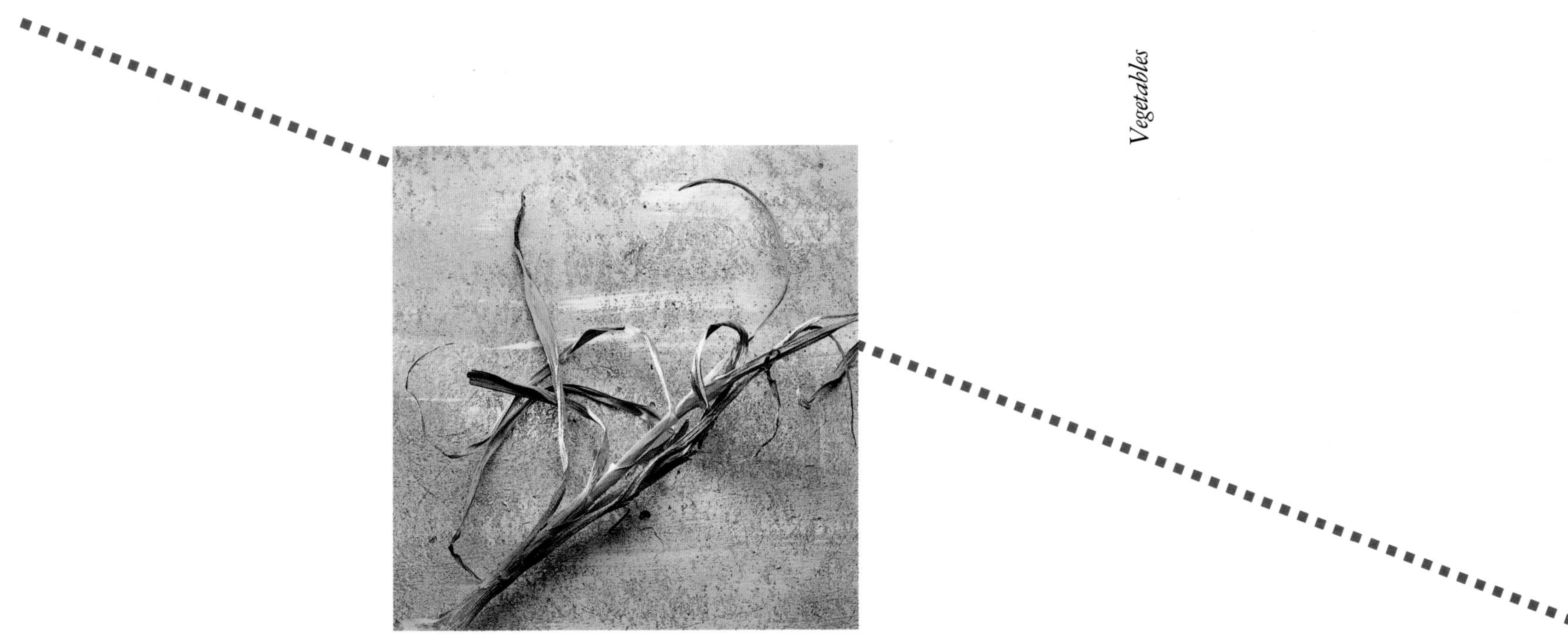

MIXED VEGETABLE GRILL

A mixed platter of vegetables satisfies the eye and the appetite. Most vegetables grill well if brushed with olive oil or butter. Allow about 1 lb / 450 g of vegetables per person - any leftovers make a wonderful grilled salad the next day.

Here are some of my favorites. Those that benefit from being marinated in seasoned olive oil, or in olive oil and lemon juice, before grilling are marked with an asterisk. Marinate for 30 - 60 minutes.

ARTICHOKES*

Remove the tough outer leaves, cut in halves or quarters, and boil in salted water until half cooked, then grill; if small, trim off the outer leaves and grill whole

BELL PEPPERS (GREEN, RED, OR YELLOW)*

Remove the core and seeds, and cut into chunks or strips

EGGPLANTS (AUBERGINES)*

Cut into thick slices if large, or grill whole if small

FENNEL*

Cut into halves, quarters, or thick slices

LETTUCES (ROMAINE/COS, ENDIVE, RADDICHIO, ETC.)*

Cut into halves or quarters, depending on size, or grill whole if small

MUSHROOMS (VARIOUS)*

Use caps only for stuffing, or grill whole

SQUASH (VARIOUS)*

Cut into chunks or thick slices

SWEETCORN ON THE COB

Remove the leaves and grill whole

TOMATOES

Cut in half if large, or grill whole if small

ZUCCHINI (COURGETTES)*

Cut into chunks if large, or grill whole if small

GRILLED MIXED LETTUCES

Choose baby lettuces (romaine/cos, butterhead endive/frise, radicchio, lollo rosso, etc.), allowing 2 per person.

1 *Depending on their size, cut the lettuces in halves or quarters, and roll them well in olive oil seasoned with salt and pepper, or in Basic Vinaigrette (see recipe page 44), or in Lemon Mustard Dressing (see recipe page 54). Marinate for 1 hour.*

2 *Drain the lettuces and reserve the marinade. Place the lettuces on an oiled grill over a medium heat. Cook for 3 - 5 minutes until golden and somewhat wilted, turning several times and basting with the rest of the marinade.*

Grilled lettuces are delicious served with cheeses such as Roquefort or Dolcelatte.

OKRA WITH MUSTARD GLAZE

1 1/2 - 2 lb / 700 - 900 g firm, fresh baby okra

MUSTARD GLAZE

1 cup / 225 g butter

4 tablespoons Dijon mustard

salt and freshly ground pepper

soaked bamboo skewers

1 *Remove the stalks from the okra and thread them onto skewers.*

2 *Melt the butter and stir in the mustard, salt, and pepper. Keep the mixture warm on the side of the grill.*

3 *Place the skewers on an oiled grill over a medium heat. Cook until slightly browned and crisp, brushing occasionally with the mustard glaze.*

Okra can also be served with Herbed Butter (see recipes pages 90 and 116) or Basic Vinaigrette (see recipe page 44).

❦ **SERVES 6**

GRILLED JERUSALEM ARTICHOKES

- 2 lbs / 900 g Jerusalem artichokes, well scrubbed
- 4 tablespoons olive oil
- salt and freshly ground pepper
- 6 tablespoons Basic Vinaigrette (see recipe page 44) - optional

1 *Boil the artichokes in salted water until half done. Drain and cool.*

2 *Season the olive oil with salt and pepper, pour it over the artichokes, and toss well.*

3 *Place the artichokes on an oiled grill over a medium heat. Cook until crisp, tender, and golden.*
Pour the vinaigrette over them, if using, and serve hot. Alternatively, allow them to marinate in vinaigrette for an hour or so and then serve at room temperature.

❦ **SERVES 6**

EGGPLANT SLICES WITH PESTO

PESTO, A SAUCE MADE FROM BASIL, OLIVE OIL, AND GARLIC, IS SOLD IN MOST GOOD DELICATESSEN STORES.

- 4 tablespoons olive oil
- salt and freshly ground pepper
- 3 lbs / 1.3 kg small eggplants (aubergines), cut lengthwise into slices 1/2 inch / 1 cm thick
- 3/4 cup / 175 ml pesto

1 *Season the olive oil with salt and pepper to taste. Brush both sides of the eggplant slices with the seasoned oil.*

2 *Place the eggplant slices on an oiled grill over a medium heat. Cook for about 4 minutes on each side until browned (not blackened).*

3 *While the eggplant slices are still hot, brush them with pesto. Serve with the rest of the pesto.*

If you prefer, you could brush the hot eggplant slices with Zhoug Mayonnaise - this is easily made by mixing 1 cup / 225 ml good mayonnaise with 1 - 2 tablespoons Zhoug Relish (see recipe page 23). Hot eggplant slices are also delicious marinated for a few hours in Zhoug-flavored vinaigrette - this is made by mixing 1 tablespoon Zhoug Relish with 1/2 cup / 100 ml Basic Vinaigrette (see recipe page 44).

❦ **SERVES 6**

GRILLED BABY EGGPLANTS

MARINADE

1/2 cup / 100 ml olive oil
1 tablespooon coarse salt
freshly ground pepper
2 tablespoons fresh rosemary

20 eggplants (aubergines) 2 - 3 inches / 5 - 7 cm long
soaked bamboo skewers

1 *Mix together the marinade ingredients.*

2 *Wash and dry the eggplants, removing the stems. Pour the marinade over them. Set aside for 2 hours, turning occasionally.*

3 *Remove the eggplants from the marinade and reserve the marinade. Thread the eggplants onto skewers. Place the skewers on an oiled grill over a medium heat and cook for about 10 minutes, turning occasionally and brushing with the reserved marinade.*

❦ **SERVES 6 OR 7**

CORN ON THE COB WITH LIME BUTTER

LIME BUTTER

1/2 cup / 100 g butter
juice and grated zest of 1 or 2 limes
cayenne pepper, to taste
salt and freshly ground pepper

12 cobs sweetcorn (2 per person), young, fresh and without leaves

1 *Melt the butter and add the lime juice and zest, cayenne, salt, and pepper. Keep the mixture warm on the side of the grill.*

2 *Brush the sweetcorn with the Lime Butter and place on the grill over a medium heat. Cook for 5 - 10 minutes or until the corn is tender and slightly charred, turning occasionally and basting with more Lime Butter. Serve with the remaining Lime Butter and extra salt and pepper.*

❦ **SERVES 6**

ZUCCHINI, SCALLIONS, AND RADICCHIO

MARINADE

- juice and grated zest of 1 orange
- juice and grated zest of 1 lemon
- 4 tablespoons olive oil
- 3 tablespoons chopped parsley
- 3 tablespoons chopped fresh basil, thyme, or coriander
- 6 cloves garlic or 2 shallots, chopped
- 1 teaspoon salt
- 1 teaspoon freshly ground pepper

- 6 zucchini (courgettes), scraped with a fork
- 12 scallions (green or spring onions)
- 3 heads radicchio, cut in half lengthwise

- soaked bamboo skewers - optional

1 *Mix together the marinade ingredients and pour over the vegetables. Toss well. Marinate for at least 1 hour.*

2 *Remove the vegetables from the marinade. Reserve the marinade. Skewer the vegetables, if desired, and cook on an oiled grill over a medium heat for about 4 minutes, turning once and brushing with the reserved marinade.*

❦ **SERVES 6**

ASPARAGUS SPEARS

- 4 - 6 fresh asparagus spears per person
- 6 tablespoons olive oil
- salt and freshly ground pepper
- 1 lemon

1 *Trim off the tough white ends of the asparagus and scrape off the skin near the cut ends.*

2 *Season the olive oil with salt and pepper. Pour over the asparagus and toss well.*

3 *Place the asparagus spears on an oiled grill over a medium heat. Cook until the spears are lightly charred, crisp, and tender, turning occasionally. Serve with a sqeeze of lemon juice, and a little olive oil, if desired.*

GRILLED BABY CARROTS

Choose small new carrots, allowing at least 3 per person.

Parboil the carrots in salted water first, then place them on an oiled grill over a medium heat for about 10 minutes, turning occasionally and basting with Chili Lime Butter (see recipe page 131), Lemon Mustard Dressing (see recipe page 54), Mint Honey Sauce (see recipe page 54), or with seasoned oil. They should be golden, crisp, and tender when cooked.

GRILLED ARTICHOKES

MARINADE

1/2 cup / 100 ml olive oil
4 cloves garlic, chopped
1 - 2 teaspoons coarse salt
1 tablespoon crumbled fresh rosemary, thyme, or oregano
1 - 2 teaspoons freshly ground pepper

6 medium globe artichokes
2 teaspoons salt
1 lemon, cut into quarters
melted butter, or mayonnaise, or Lemon Mustard Dressing (see recipe page 54), or Basic Vinaigrette (see recipe page 44)

1 *Mix together the marinade ingredients and set aside.*

2 *Cut the artichokes in halves or quarters. Bring a large saucepan of water to a boil, adding the salt and quarters of lemon. Add the artichokes and bring to a boil again. Lower the heat and simmer for 10 - 12 minutes or until the artichokes are almost tender Drain and allow to cool a little. Remove the fluffy parts (chokes) of the artichokes. Pour the marinade over the artichokes and toss well. Marinate for 1 hour.*

3 *Remove the artichokes from the marinade and reserve the marinade. Place on an oiled grill over a low heat. Cook for 15 - 20 minutes, basting with the reserved marinade. Serve hot or at room temperature with melted butter, mayonnaise, Lemon Mustard Dressing, or Basic Vinaigrette.*

❦ **SERVES 6**

GRILLED POTATOES

6 tablespoons olive oil
coarse salt and freshly ground pepper
12 small potatoes, well scrubbed

1 *Mix the olive oil, salt, and pepper to a paste, and roll the potatoes in it.*

2 *Remove the potatoes from the oil and place them on an oiled grill over a medium low heat. Cook for 25 - 30 minutes or until lightly charred, turning occasionally and brushing with the rest of the seasoned oil. Keep the potatoes warm until ready to serve.*

Larger potatoes can be cooked in the same way. Parboil them in their skins first, pat them dry, and proceed as above. They will take about 30 minutes to cook right through.

❦ **SERVES 6**

SWEET POTATOES WITH CHILI LIME BUTTER

2 lbs / 900 g sweet potatoes, well scrubbed

CHILI LIME BUTTER

1 cup / 225 g butter

juice and grated zest of 1 lime

chili pepper flakes

salt and freshly ground pepper

1 *Boil the sweet potatoes in salted water until half cooked. Drain and cool them, then slice them lengthwise into slices 1/2 inch / 1 cm thick.*

2 *Melt the butter and cook over a low heat until it browns and begins to smell nutty. Season with the lime juice and zest, and with chili flakes, and salt and pepper to taste.*

3 *Brush the sweet potatoes slices with the Chili Lime Butter and place on an oiled grill over a medium heat. Cook until crisp, golden brown, and tender, turning once or twice and basting with more Chili Lime Butter. Serve with any remaining Chili Lime Butter*

❦ **SERVES 6**

GRILLED POTATO SLICES

1/2 cup / 100 ml olive oil

4 - 6 cloves garlic, chopped

salt and freshly ground pepper

3 lbs potatoes / 1.3 kg, well scrubbed

1 cup / 225 ml good mayonnaise

2 - 3 tablespoons pesto (see note page 125), or Zhoug Relish (see recipe page 23), or olivada (olive sauce, available in most good delicatessen stores)

1 *Combine the olive oil, garlic, salt, and pepper, and set aside.*

2 *Cook the potatoes in boiling salted water until half cooked. Drain and cool slightly. Cut each potato into slices 1/2 inch / 1 cm thick, pour the seasoned oil over them, and marinate for 2 hours or overnight.*

3 *Place the potato slices on an oiled grill over a medium heat. Cook on both sides until crisp, brown, and tender. Serve with mayonnaise mixed with pesto, or with Zhoug Relish, or olivada.*

Any mayonnaise-based sauce is delicious with these crisp potato slices. They are also very good with *aioli* (garlic mayonnaise) or with *rouille* (a Provençal sauce made from chilis, garlic, breadcrumbs, oil, and stock).

❦ **SERVES 6**

GRILLED FENNEL

Fennel bulbs can be grilled in quarters or thick slices.

Allow one large bulb per person.

Place on an oiled grill over a medium low heat (at the side of the grill, for example) and cook for 15 - 20 minutes until crisp, tender, and lightly charred. Turn occasionally and baste with Herbed Butter (see recipes pages 90 and 116), Lemon Mustard Dressing (see recipe page 54), or seasoned olive oil.

MIXED MUSHROOMS

MARINADE

- 1/2 cup / 100 ml olive oil
- 2 tablespoons red wine, sherry, or balsamic vinegar
- 4 cloves garlic, minced
- 2 tablespoons chopped fresh thyme or oregano

- 1 1/2 lbs / 700 g mushrooms (field, button, shitake, oyster, etc.)
- soaked bamboo skewers - optional
- 3 tablespoons chopped parsley
- salt and freshly ground pepper

1 *Mix together the marinade ingredients.*

2 *Clean the mushrooms with a damp cloth. Pour the marinade over them and set aside for at least 1 hour.*

3 *Remove the mushrooms from the marinade. Skewer them or place them directly on an oiled grill over a medium heat. Cook for 2 - 3 minutes until golden and tender. Serve sprinkled with parsley, salt, and pepper.*

SERVES 6

GRILLED GARLIC

whole bulbs of garlic, unpeeled
olive oil.

Soak the garlic in warm water for 30 minutes, then marinate it in olive oil for 1 hour. Grill over a low heat for 25 - 30 minutes until soft.

GRILLED SHALLOTS

Shallots should be prepared in the same way as garlic - soaked unpeeled in warm water, then marinated in olive oil for an hour or so. Grill over a low heat for 10 - 15 minutes.

RED ONION SLICES

5 - 6 large sweet red onions (large white onions will do, but they are less attractive)
6 tablespoons olive oil
salt and freshly ground pepper

1 *Peel the onions and cut them into rounds 1/2 inch / 1 cm thick. Season with salt and pepper, and brush with olive oil.*

2 *Place the onion slices on an oiled grill over a medium heat. Cook until golden and tender, turning a few times and basting with more olive oil.*

❦ **SERVES 6**

GRILLED LEEKS

12 small leeks
6 tablespoons olive oil
salt and freshly ground pepper
fresh oregano, thyme, or rosemary

1 *Trim all but 2 inches / 5 cm of the green off the leeks. Slit them lengthwise to within 1 inch / 2.5 cm of their base. Rinse under cold water to remove any soil. Blanch in boiling salted water until just tender. Drain and rinse immediately in cold water. Drain again.*

2 *Season the oil with the salt, pepper, and herbs, pour over the leeks, and toss well. Marinate for 1 hour.*

3 *Remove the leeks from the marinade, reserving the marinade. Place the leeks on an oiled grill over a medium low heat. Cook for 3 - 4 minutes, turning several times and brushing with the reserved marinade.*

Leeks can also be marinated in Basic Vinaigrette (see recipe page 44) or in Lemon Mustard Dressing (see recipe page 54), or prepared as above and then marinated in either and served at room temperature. Scallions (green or spring onions) can be prepared in the same way.

❦ **SERVES 6**

Fruit

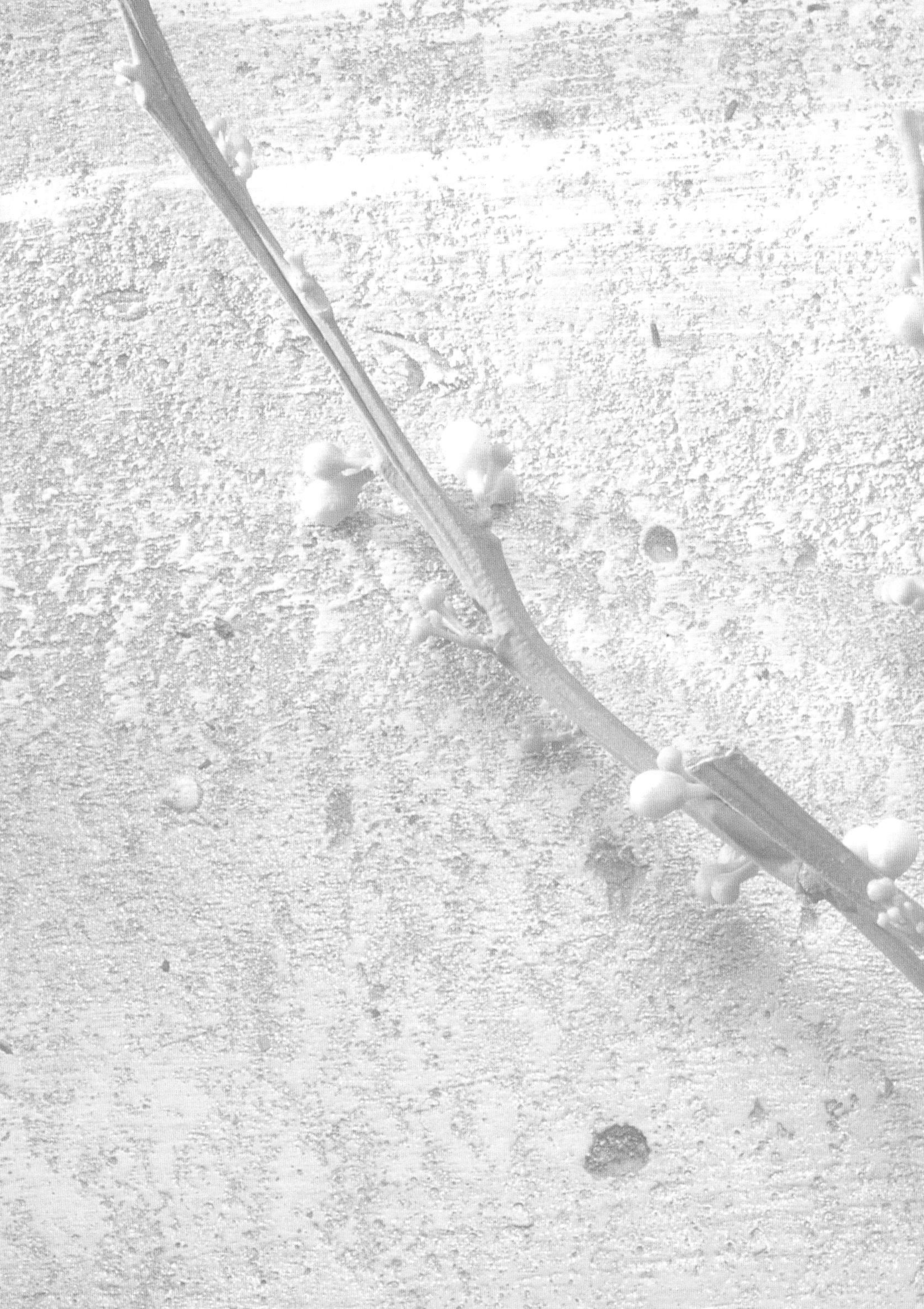

Jews and Christians are convinced that Adam and Eve wore out their welcome in the Garden of Eden when they ate an apple. Polynesian Islanders are quite sure that it was a banana they ate; descendants of the Carib Indians are firm in their belief that it was a papaya; and Trobriand Islanders are certain that it was a pineapple. Since the beginning of time, men and women have always been in trouble because of one fruit or another.

Margaret Mead

American anthropologist

(1901 - 1978)

CHAPTER EIGHT

Fruit

The roles traditionally reserved for fruit are the dessert and the snack between meals. But fruit has enormous potential as an accompaniment to meat, poultry, and fish, and yet another career as a companion to vegetables, cheese, and smoked meat appetizers.

❦ *When buying fruit for grilling, always select fine quality, unbruised fruits that are ripe and firm. Before grilling, thoroughly scrub the grill rack with a wire brush to remove any adhering fragments of meat or fish that might spoil the flavor.*

❦ *Fruit is best grilled over coals that have passed their fiercest heat, so place them on the grill after the main course has been cooked.*

RECIPES

Fruit

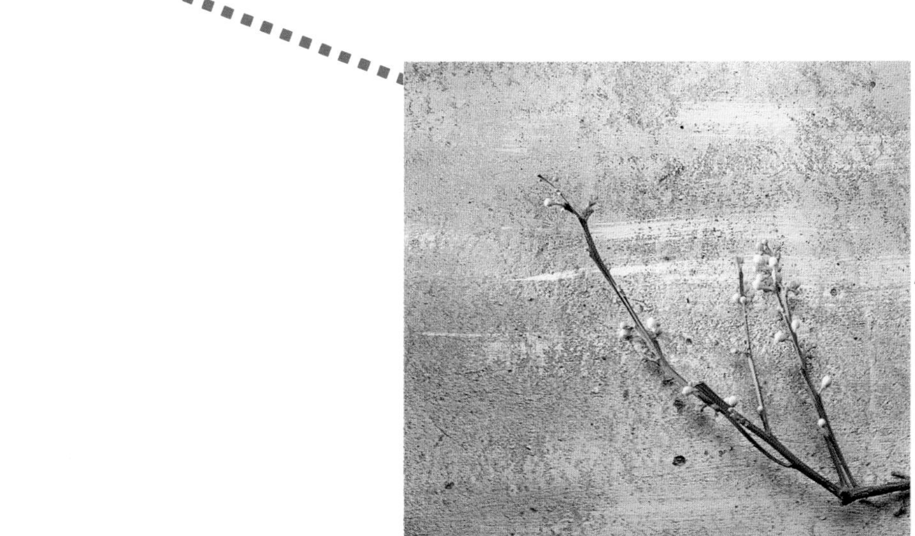

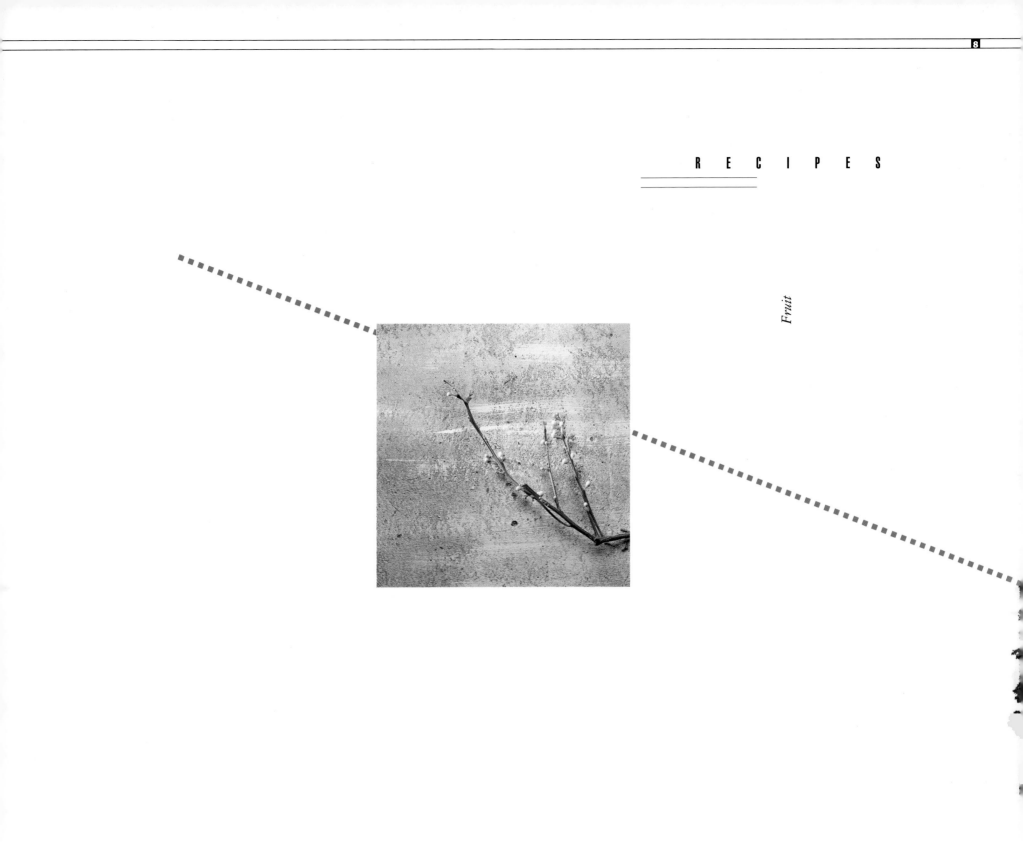

PEARS WITH ROQUEFORT CHEESE

FRUIT MARINADE
1/2 cup / 100 ml fresh orange juice
1/2 cup / 100 ml blueberry, raspberry, or other fruit vinegar
6 tablespoons walnut, olive, or vegetable oil
6 tablespoons apricot preserve or marmalade

6 large pears (ripe but firm)
12 oz / 350 g Roquefort cheese

1 *To make the marinade, mix together the orange juice and vinegar, then beat in the oil and preserve or marmalade.*

2 *Cut the pears in half and remove the cores, but do not peel them. Pour the marinade over them and set aside for at least 2 hours.*

3 *Remove the pears from the marinade, reserving the marinade. Place the pears on an oiled grill over a medium low heat. Cook until golden, turning and basting with the reserved marinade. Serve hot with slices of Roquefort cheese.*

❦ **SERVES 6**

HONEY PEACHES

1/3 cup / 75 g butter
2 tablespoons honey
1 - 2 tablespoons lemon or lime juice - optional
6 large peaches

1 *Melt the butter and stir in the honey. Add lemon or lime juice for sharpness, if liked.*

2 *Peel the peaches, cut them in half, and take the stones out. Dip the peach halves in the melted butter mixture and place on an oiled grill over a low heat. Cook until golden brown, turning and brushing frequently with the rest of the butter mixture.*

❦ **SERVES 6**

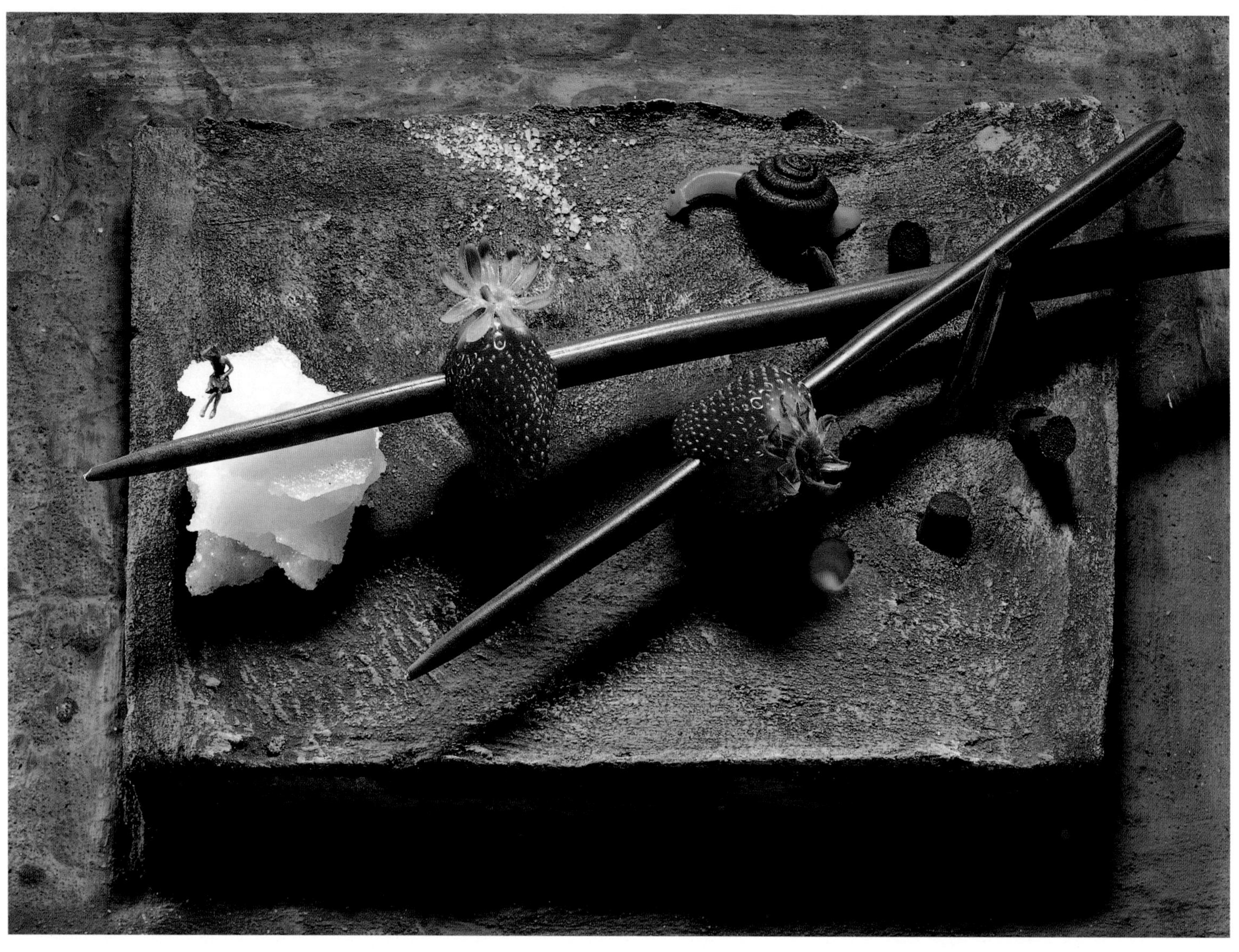

BROCHETTES OF SUMMER FRUITS

- 1 small cantaloupe melon, peeled and seeded
- 3 ripe plums, halved and skinned
- 3 small ripe peaches, halved and skinned
- 1 ripe papaya (pawpaw), peeled and seeded
- 12 large whole strawberries
- juice of 1 lemon
- Fruit Marinade (see recipe page 141 or 146) - optional
- soaked bamboo skewers
- 1/2 cup / 100 ml Sweet Lime Butter (see recipe page 146) - optional

1 *Cut the melon and papaya into 12 pieces. Sprinkle all the cut fruits with lemon juice to prevent them from discoloring, or marinate them for at least 2 hours in the Fruit Marinade of your choice.*

2 *Remove the fruit from the marinade, if using, and reserve the marinade. Thread two pieces of melon and papaya, two strawberries, and half a plum and peach onto each skewer to make 6 brochettes. Place on an oiled grill over a low heat. Cook until golden and lightly singed, basting with the reserved marinade or with Sweet Lime Butter. Serve the brochettes on their own, or with a fruit sorbet or vanilla ice cream.*

❦ **SERVES 6**

FRESH DATES WITH HONEY AND CREAM

- 1/2 cup / 100 g butter
- juice of 1/2 lemon
- 2 tablespoons honey
- 2 - 2 1/2 lbs / 0.9 - 1.2 kg fresh yellow dates on the stalk
- 2 cups / 450 ml whipped cream
- extra honey

1 *Melt the butter and stir in the lemon juice and honey. Remove from the heat.*

2 *Place the dates on an oiled grill over a medium low heat. Brush well with the butter, lemon, and honey mixture, and cook until golden and sizzling, turning several times.*

3 *Serve with a bowl of whipped cream and a bowl of honey for dipping.*

❦ **SERVES 6 TO 8**

GRILLED COCONUT

- 1 fresh coconut
- 2 - 3 tablespoons honey
- 4 tablespoons tequila
- juice of 2 limes
- 1/2 tablespoon grated zest of lime
- lime sorbet - optional

1 *Break the coconut open, remove the meat, and cut it into large chunks.*

2 *Mix together the honey, tequila, lime juice, and lime zest. Pour the mixture over the coconut chunks and marinate for 30 minutes.*

3 *Remove the coconut from the marinade and reserve the marinade. Place the coconut chunks on an oiled grill over a low heat and grill for 5 - 10 minutes, basting with the reserved marinade. Serve hot or cold, with a sorbet and the rest of the marinade.*

SERVES 4 TO 6

MIXED MELONS

- assorted melons (1 cantaloupe, 1/2 casaba melon, and 1/2 honeydew, for example)
- Fruit Marinade (see recipe page 141 or 146)

1 *Cut the melons into thick slices or wedges, removing the seeds. Allow two or three slices/wedges per person. Marinate for at least 2 hours in the Fruit Marinade of your choice.*

2 *Remove the melon slices from the marinade and reserve the marinade. Place on an oiled grill over a low heat. Cook until golden brown, turning and basting occasionally with the reserved marinade.*

SERVES 6

MANGO WITH SWEET LIME BUTTER

3 large ripe mangoes
SWEET LIME BUTTER
1/2 cup / 100 g butter
1 tablespoon honey
juice and grated zest of 1 lime

1 *Peel the mangoes, remove the fibrous stones, and cut the flesh into thick wedges.*

2 *Melt the butter over a low heat and continue to cook until it begins to brown and smell nutty. Stir in the honey, lime juice, and zest.*

3 *Place the mango wedges on an oiled grill over a medium low heat. Cook until golden brown, turning occasionally and basting with the Sweet Lime Butter. Serve with the remaining Sweet Lime Butter.*

❦ **SERVES 4**

PEACHES, NECTARINES, AND APRICOTS

3 firm ripe peaches
3 firm ripe nectarines
3 firm ripe apricots
FRUIT MARINADE
6 tablespoons peach or apricot juice/nectar
2 tablespoons fresh lemon juice
6 tablespoons fruit vinegar
3 tablespoons walnut or other nut oil
4 tablespoons peach or apricot preserve
vanilla ice cream - optional

1 *Halve the fruit and remove the stones, but do not peel.*

2 *To make the marinade, mix together the peach or apricot juice, lemon juice, and vinegar, then beat in the oil and preserve.*

3 *Pour the marinade over the fruit and toss well. Marinate for at least 2 hours.*

4 *Remove the fruit from the marinade and reserve the marinade. Place the fruit on an oiled grill over a low heat. Cook, basting occasionally with the reserved marinade, until golden brown. Serve with vanilla ice cream, if desired.*

❦ **SERVES 6**

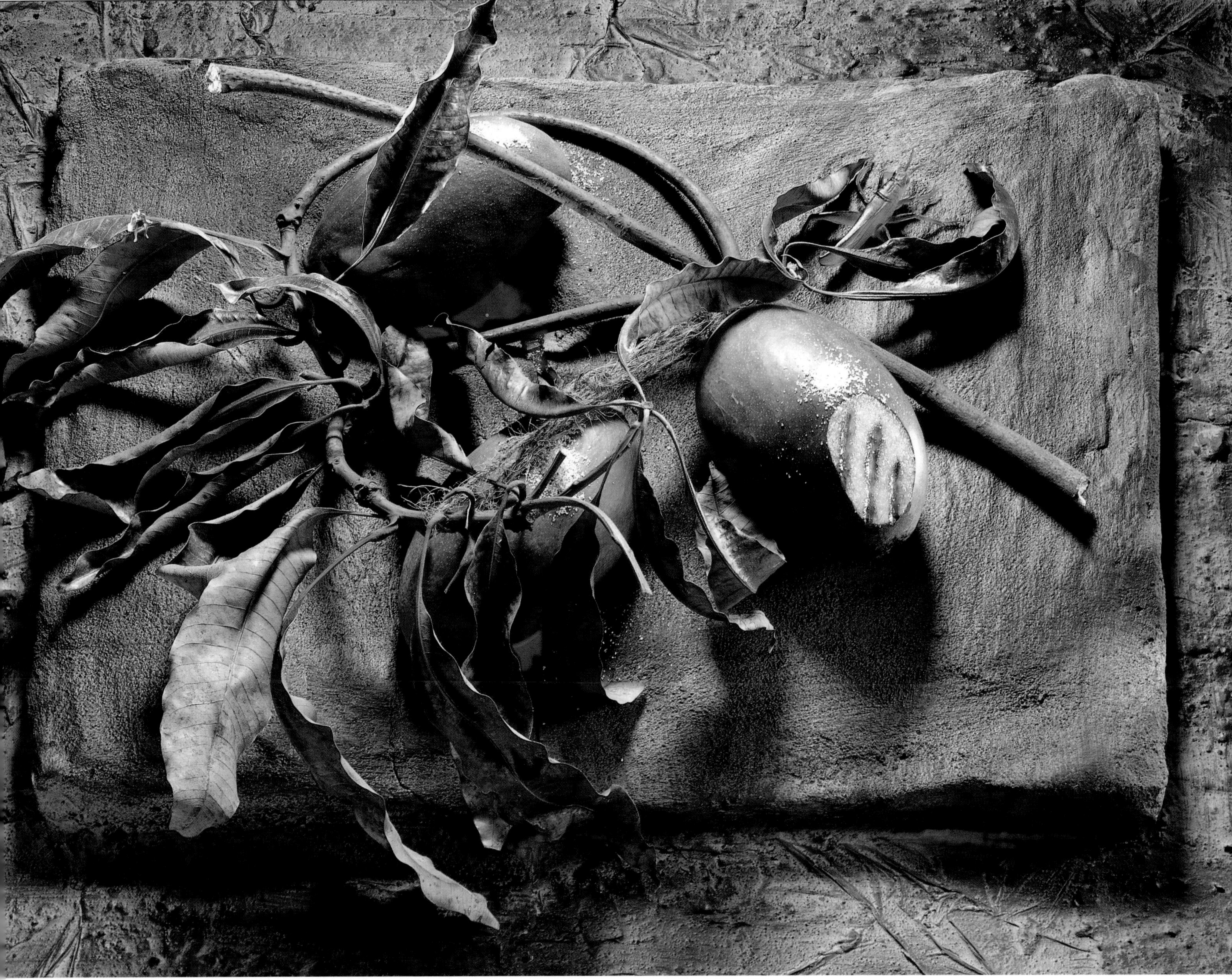

FRESH FIGS WITH CASSIS CREAM

- 18 - 24 firm fresh figs, halved
- soaked bamboo skewers
- 6 tablespoons melted butter
- 1 1/2 cups / 325 ml cream
- 2 tablespoons cassis (blackcurrant) liqueur
- sprigs of fresh mint, to garnish

1 *Thread the figs onto skewers and place on an oiled grill over a medium low heat. Cook, turning and basting with the melted butter, until golden.*

2 *Beat the cassis liqueur into the cream. Pour over the figs or pour into serving bowls and place the figs on top. Garnish with mint sprigs.*

❦ **SERVES 6**

GRILLED PINEAPPLE

- 1 large pineapple
- 4 tablespoons honey
- 1/3 cup / 75 g butter

1 *Peel the pineapple and cut it into rounds or wedges 1 inch / 2.5 cm thick. Melt the butter, stir in the honey, and pour over the pineapple. Marinate for at least 1 hour.*

2 *Remove the pineapple from the marinade, reserving the marinade. Place on an oiled grill over a medium low heat. Cook until golden, turning and brushing with the reserved marinade.*

❦ **SERVES 5 OR 6**

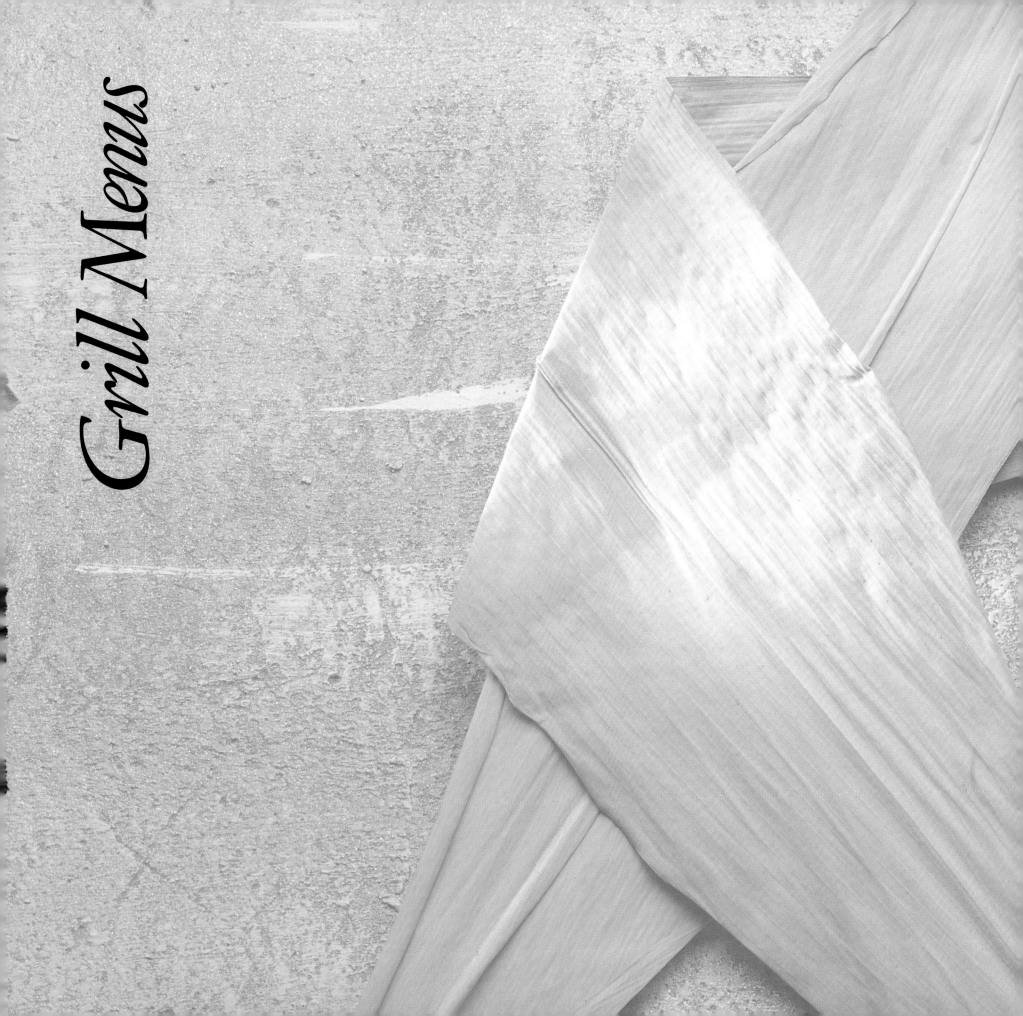

Grill Menus

ALL HUMAN HISTORY ATTESTS

THAT HAPPINESS FOR MAN -

THE HUNGRY SINNER -

SINCE EVE ATE APPLES,

MUCH DEPENDS ON DINNER!

Lord Byron

English poet

(1788 - 1824)

CHAPTER NINE

Grill Menus

Recently, anticipating a quiet evening at home and nothing more strenuous than a little reading, a late night snack and, if the mood was right, half a bottle of wine, things began to go "agley," as Robbie Burns would have said. At seven in the evening the doorbell rang. Within the space of the next hour or so, it rang again, and again. By half past eight, four adult males, three adult females, and several young children had presented themselves. And they were all hungry.

❦ *It took only a few minutes to prepare the grill and think up a menu based on the vegetables in the larder, the two small fish and one pork tenderloin in the fridge, and the fruit in the fruitbowl. The evening was unexpected and unplanned, but it turned into a delightful occasion with delightful people.*

❦ *Grill cooking is enormously flexible. Because so many possibilities exist, it is not difficult to think up a menu for almost any occasion. Although some things are important - such as top quality ingredients - formality hardly ever is. Whether you decide to serve an appetizer as a main course, or a large fish as an appetizer, or the soup before the appetizer, or a salad before the main course, pleasure and fun come first.*

❦ *The menus that follow are only suggestions. There are no sacred cows when it comes to grill menus. If you are the chef, you are the boss.*

RECIPES

Grill Menus

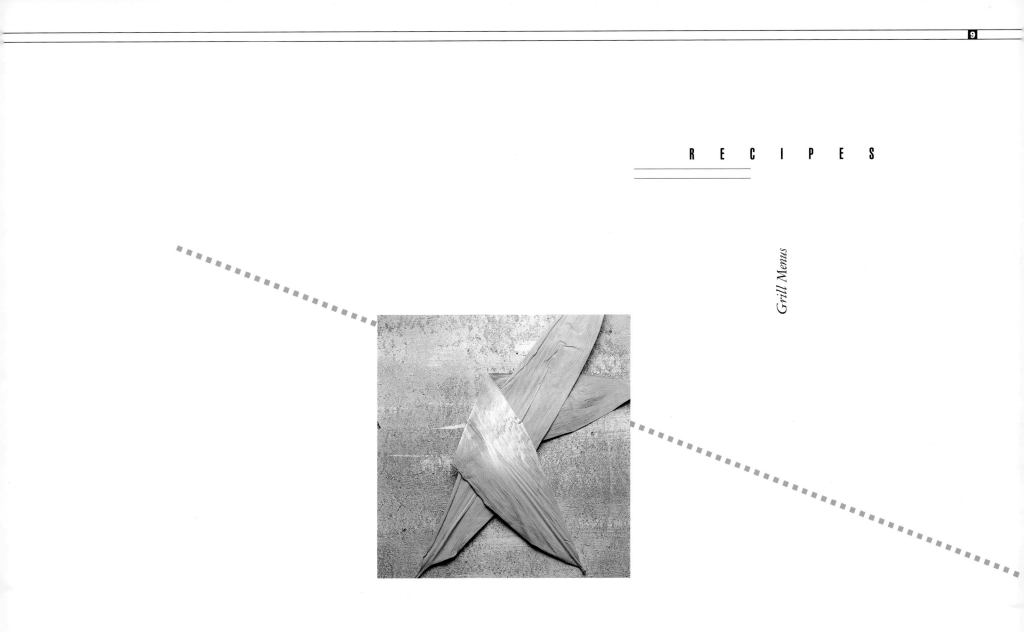

EXCLUSIVELY HORS D'OEUVRES

Skewered Chicken with Scallions	*p* **27**
Okra with Mustard Glaze	*p* **124**
Skewers of Salmon	*p* **20**
Mixed Mushrooms	*p* **132**
Papaya Skewers with Chili Lime Butter	*p* **24**
Chili Prawns with Coriander Dipping Sauce	*p* **24**

❦

Suggested beverages: plenty of chilled beer and wine, fresh fruit juices, and a house drink such as Daiquiri, Margarita, or Mai Tai.

❦

A BEACH PARTY CLAMBAKE

Clams and Mussels with Herbed Butter	*p* **41**

❦

Garden Salad with Lemon Mustard Dressing	*p* **54**

❦

Grilled Lobsters	*p* **79**
Lemon Pepper Chicken	*p* **27**
Corn on the Cob with Lime Butter	*p* **126**
Grilled Potatoes	*p* **130**
Herbed Garlic Bread	*p* **30**

❦

Watermelon

❦

DINNER IN A RUSTIC MOOD

Eggplant and Chili Soup	*p* **41**
Herbed Garlic Bread	*p* **30**
❦	
Butterflied Leg of Lamb	*p* **112**
Grilled Leeks	*p* **134**
Grilled Artichokes	*p* **129**
Grilled Potatoes	*p* **130**
Grilled Baby Carrots	*p* **128**
❦	
Fresh Dates with Honey and Cream	*p* **143**
❦	

AN ELEGANT DINNER PARTY

Skewered Chicken with Cherry Tomatoes	*p* **27**
Okra with Mustard Glaze	*p* **124**
Grilled Scallions	*p* **134**
❦	
Grilled Scallops	*p* **82**
Herbed Garlic Bread with basil and chives	*p* **30**
❦	
Whole Salmon with Herb and Lemon Salsa	*p* **73**
Corn on the Cob with Lime Butter	*p* **126**
Mushrooms Stuffed with Fresh Herbs	*p* **23**
❦	
Lettuce and Arugula Salad with Lemon Mustard Dressing	*p* **54**
❦	
Fresh Figs with Cassis Cream	*p* **148**
❦	

A HEARTY STEAK DINNER

Soft-Shelled Crabs with Browned Butter	*p* **77**
❦	
Steaks with Mustard and Herb Crust	*p* **107**
Mushrooms Stuffed with Fresh Herbs	*p* **23**
Grilled Potato Slices with aioli	*p* **131**
Red Onion Slices	*p* **134**
❦	
Garden Salad	
Pears with Roquefort Cheese	*p* **141**
❦	

A SUMMER BRUNCH

Bruschette with Mushrooms	*p* **36**
❦	
Herbed Garlic Bread	*p* **30**
Mixed Mushrooms	*p* **132**
❦	
Cured Salmon Steaks with Herbs	*p* **72**
Okra, Corn, and Basil Salad	*p* **63**
Asparagus Spears	*p* **128**
Marinated Papaya Salad (see recipe right)	
❦	
Honey Peaches	*p* **141**
Mango with Sorbet	
❦	

MARINATED PAPAYA SALAD

1 large or 2 small firm papayas (pawpaws)

MARINADE

2 tablespoons lemon or lime juice

2 - 3 tablespoons olive oil

1/2 - 1 teaspoon coarse salt

10 - 15 drops tabasco sauce, or to taste

freshly ground pepper

1 *Peel the fruit and discard the seeds. Using a hand grater or the grating disk of a food processor, grate the papaya into thin strips.*

2 *Mix together the marinade ingredients, pour over the papaya and toss well. Marinate for at least 30 minutes before serving.*

❦ **SERVES 4** AS A STARTER OR SIDE DISH

AN ASIAN EVENING

Crabs with Black Bean Sauce	p **79**
❦	
Pork Tenderloin Southeast-Asian Style	p **117**
Eggplant Slices with Zhoug Mayonnaise	p **125**
Papaya Skewers with Chili Lime Butter	p **24**
Asparagus Spears	p **128**
❦	
Mango with Sweet Lime Butter	p **146**
❦	

A FAMILY COOKOUT

Mixed Sausage Grill	p **110**
❦	
Hamburgers with Roquefort Cheese	p **109**
Corn on the Cob with Lime Butter	p **126**
Grilled Potato Slices	p **131**
Red Onion Slices	p **134**
❦	
Garden Salad	
❦	
Hot Fudge Sundae	
❦	

A LIGHT SPRING LUNCHEON

Artichoke Soup	p **36**
Bruschette (Version 1)	p **30**
❦	
Tuna Salad	p **63**
❦	
Fresh Fruit	
Selection of Cheeses	
❦	

LIGHT FARE FOR SUMMER

Grilled Lettuces with Feta Cheese	*p* **48**
Herbed Garlic Bread	*p* **30**
❦	
Grilled Red Snapper with Herb and Lemon Salsa	*p* **73**
Julienne of Hearts of Palm (see recipe below right)	
Corn on the Cob with Lime Butter	*p* **126**
Grilled Fennel	*p* **132**
❦	
Peaches, Nectarines, and Apricots	*p* **146**
❦	

A SEAFOOD COCKTAIL PARTY

Grilled Scallops	*p* **82**
Skewers of Salmon	*p* **20**
Chili Prawns with Coriander Dipping Sauce	*p* **24**
Oysters with Mignonette Sauce	*p* **42**
Clams with Black Bean Sauce	*pp* **41** & **79**
Mussels with Chili Vinaigrette	*p* **44**
Swordfish Skewers	*p* **23**
❦	

A SPRING LAMB DINNER

Whole Fish with Fresh Herbs	*p* **72**
Bruschette (Version 2)	*p* **30**
❦	
Loin Lamb Chops	*p* **110**
Grilled Jerusalem Artichokes	*p* **125**
Grilled Garlic and Shallots	*p* **134**
Eggplant Slices with Pesto	*p* **125**
❦	
Fresh Figs with Cassis Cream	*p* **148**
❦	

JULIENNE OF HEARTS OF PALM

- 10 oz / 300 g hearts of palm, drained
- 3 - 5 tablespoons dry white wine
- 1 - 2 tablespoons olive oil
- 3 tablespoons snipped chives or finely chopped scallions (spring onions)

1 *With your hands, shred the hearts of palm lengthwise into thin strips.*

2 *Mix together the rest of the ingredients, pour over the palm hearts, and toss well. Allow to stand for at least 1 hour before serving.*

❦ **SERVES 4** AS A SIDE DISH

PICNIC FARE

This menu is intended to be prepared at home and taken to the picnic site to be eaten cold.

Tomato Soup with Herbs *p* **38**

❦

Lemon Pepper Chicken *p* **27**

❦

Grilled Turkey Breast *p* **97**

Artichoke, Fennel, and Potato Salad *p* **64**

Okra, Corn, and Basil Salad *p* **63**

Zucchini Salad *p* **63**

❦

Tropical Fruit Salad

❦

A GRILLED DINNER IN THE FALL

Scallops with Prosciutto *p* **39**

❦

Veal Chops with Sage *p* **115**

Grilled Radicchio and Lettuce *p* **124**

Mushrooms Stuffed with Fresh Herbs *p* **23**

Grilled Baby Carrots *p* **128**

❦

Honey Peaches *p* **141**

❦

Selection of Cheeses

❦

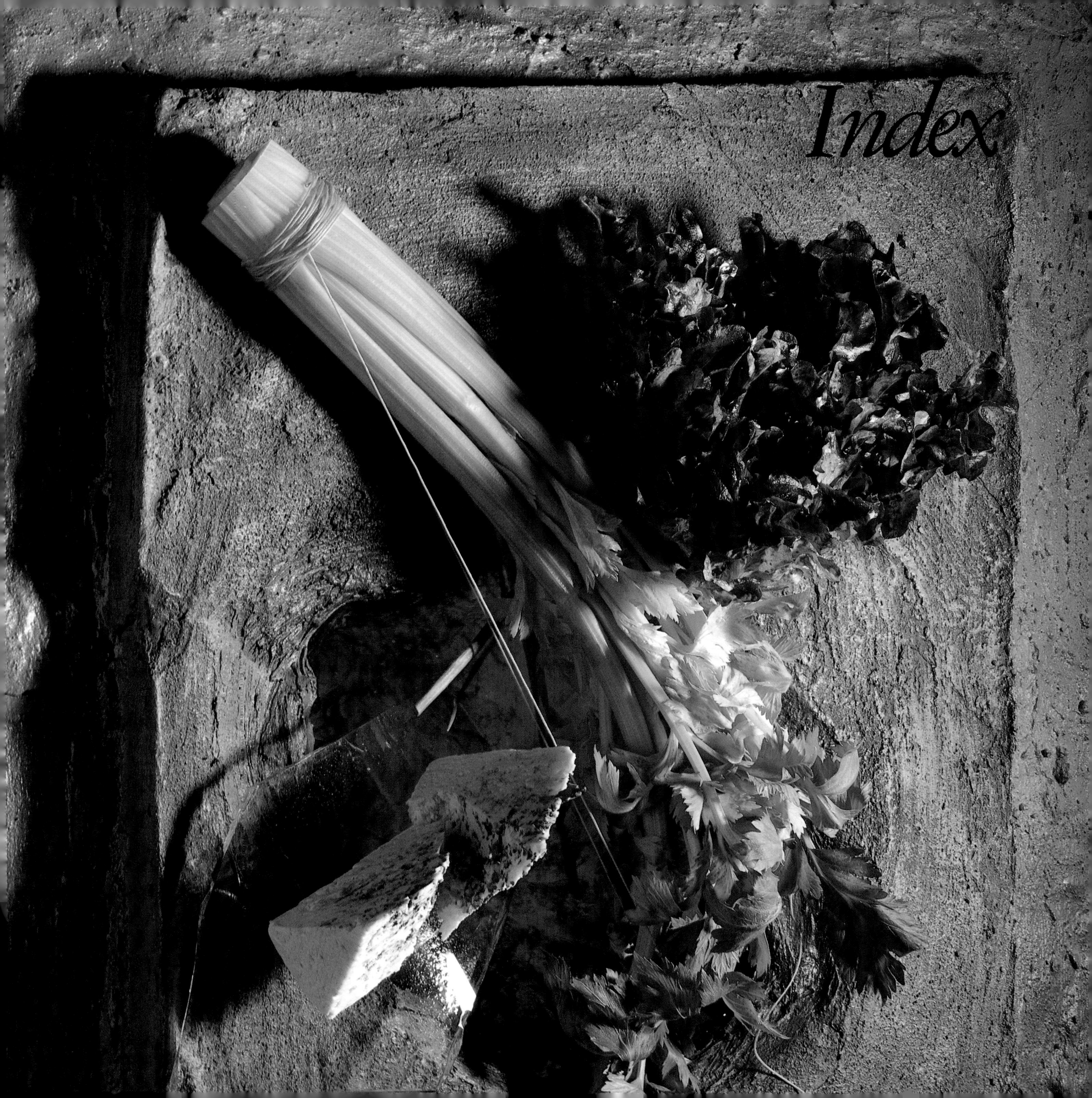
Index

F

G

H

J

L

M

O

P

R

S